Presented to:

Butler Area Public Library

In Memory of
William Post

Donor
Friends of Arby's Restaurant

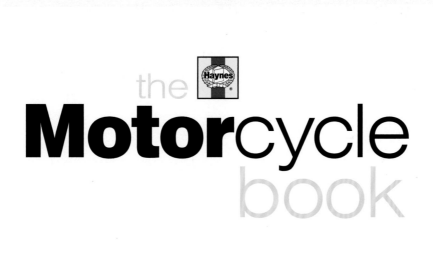

the **Motor**cycle book

© Haynes Publishing 2006

All rights reserved. No part of this publication may be
reproduced, stored in a retrieval system or
transmitted, in any form or by any means, electronic,
mechanical, photocopying, recording or otherwise,
without prior permission in writing from the publisher.

First published in September 2002
Reprinted February 2003

Second edition published in September 2006

A catalogue record for this book is
available from the British Library

ISBN 1 84425 342 2

Library of Congress catalog card no. 2006924137

Published by Haynes Publishing, Sparkford,
Yeovil, Somerset BA22 7JJ, England

Tel: +44 1963 442030 Fax: +44 1963 440001
E-mail: sales@haynes.co.uk
Website: www.haynes.co.uk

Haynes North America, Inc.,
861 Lawrence Drive, Newbury Park,
California 91320, USA

Printed and bound in England by
J. H. Haynes & Co. Ltd, Sparkford

the **Motor**cycle book

Everything you need to know
about owning, enjoying and
maintaining your bike

Second Edition

Which motorcycle?

Training

Clothing

Insurance

Security

Luggage

Tyres

Wheels

Brakes

Suspension

Frames

Engines

Tuning

Exhausts

Accessories

Electrics

MoTs

Storage

Maintenance

Trouble-shooting

Alan Seeley

1

Which motorcycle?

2

Getting **on** the road

Know your motorcycle

Looking after your motorcycle

1
Which motorcycle?

Sportsbikes

Sportsbikes are in a constant state of evolution. The manufacturers' relentless pursuit of more power from increasingly lighter and compact engines has put blistering performance in the hands of ordinary riders at affordable prices.

Two capacity groups dominate the sportsbike sector – 600cc and the litre class. With over 100bhp on tap and top speeds in the 160mph bracket, it's easy to see the appeal of the 600s – especially if your age, experience, or driving record make insurance premiums for larger capacity sportsbikes prohibitively expensive.

Racing, they say, improves the breed, and the influence of competition development can be seen in the lines and technology of many of today's superbikes. Underseat exhausts, radial brakes, slipper clutches, and mass-centralisation – where as much of the bike as possible is brought close to the centre of gravity for sharp handling – are just a few examples of manufacturers showcasing lessons learned on the race track.

As has already been said, sportsbikes can be broadly divided into 600cc and 1000cc classes, although there are a few anomalies, as we'll see.

Some 600s are less compromising than others, making them ideal choices for riders who want to explore the outer limits of their bike's performance on track as well as on road. Of the supersports 600cc four-cylinder bikes, the Yamaha R6 and, to an only slightly lesser extent, Suzuki's GSX-R600 are the most single-minded. But their ultra-sharp handling and committed riding positions can be a bit much for riders who favour straight-line stability and comfort. Their first choices would be Kawasaki's capable ZX-6R, which is actually 636cc, or Honda's CBR600, available in a comparatively 'soft' F version or in the more highly-strung 'RR' designation.

Honda CBR1000RR in-line 4-cylinder 998cc, 170bhp, 176kg   *Triumph Daytona in-line 3-cylinder 675cc, 123bhp, 165kg*

Suzuki GSX-R1000 in-line 4-cylinder 999cc, 175bhp, 166kg

A fresh contender in the class arrived in 2006 in the form of the Triumph Daytona 675. Not only is its capacity unusual, but it boasts a three-cylinder engine rather than a four, placing it somewhere between the four-cylinder 600s and the 750cc twins. With plenty of torque and fine handling it follows its own rules.

Another bike that ploughs its own furrow is the Suzuki GSX-R750. It's now much more advanced than the bike launched back in 1985, but it's still mental. Racing rules have left the four with nowhere to play in top-flight competition, but a die-hard fan base has kept the GSX-R in Suzuki's catalogue for years.

If in-line four-cylinder power isn't to your tastes, then Ducati's 749 provides a V-twin alternative with comparable power and peerless race-bred handling.

If the 100bhp+ and 160mph potential of the 600s isn't enough for you, then you'll be looking at a litre bike, seen by manufacturers and riders alike as the pinnacle of sportsbiking. The class was established by Honda's FireBlade back in 1992. Here was a bike that packed over 900cc's-worth of power from a compact engine into a nimble 600cc-size chassis. It would take six years for the competition to catch up, Yamaha eventually trumping Honda with the R1.

The current crop of 1000cc superbikes still adheres to the philosophy of the first Blade, offering a winning combination of big-bore behemoth power from compact engines in sparse chassis. Suzuki's class-leading GSX-R1000 is the perfect expression of the concept, boasting 178bhp and the same weight as a 600. The bike the GSX-R1000 deposed, Yamaha's R1, boasts better comfort than

the more focussed Suzuki. Meanwhile, the bike that started it all, the Honda Fireblade (now with a small 'B') has a little less power but remains the most ridable. Kawasaki's ZX-10R blew onto the scene a few years back and terrified riders and the competition alike with its raw aggression, but mid-decade it got a little smoother.

If you don't want a Japanese litre four, try these. MV Agusta's F4 1000S is not only gorgeous but exceptionally capable too. It carries a big price tag, though. Triumph's 955i was a Brit take on the litre theme, this time with a three-cylinder engine, but it failed to match the competition. Still, it's good on the road. Benelli's Tornado is an exotic 898cc triple, but beset by reliability issues.

Stars of the V-twin litre class are Ducati's 999, Aprilia's RSV Mille, and Honda's SP-2, all derived from race bikes designed to race in and win World Superbike Championships.

If speed is your ultimate pursuit then go hyper-sports. Suzuki's Hayabusa is a 1300cc monster that can nudge 200mph yet still take you comfortably to work and even touring. The Honda Blackbird briefly held the world's fastest road bike crown before the Hayabusa came along. Then Kawasaki built the ZX-12R to top the lot, then aced itself with the ZZ-R1400. Despite their size, any of these can be surprisingly nimble.

Whichever sportsbike you opt for, don't worry if its performance is a little beyond you on road or track – you're not alone, despite whatever Rossi-esque capabilities your mates might boast for themselves.

Suzuki's GSX-R1000 topped the superbike list when it was launched for 2001, but who knows what Honda, Yamaha and Kawasaki have up their sleeves? Sportsbikes are in a constant state of evolution.

They might sound a contradiction in terms, but today's sports-tourers really do offer a decent all-round package. They're the first choice for the rider who demands comfort for serious mile-munching in a bike that can still cut it on a Sunday blast in the twisties.

Sports-tourers

Kawasaki ZZ-R1200 in-line four, 16-valve, 1164cc, 160bhp (claimed), 236kg (dry)

Honda VFR800 Fi V4 16-valve, 781cc, 104.6bhp (claimed), 210kg (dry)

Ducati ST4s V-twin, 8-valve, 996cc, 117bhp (claimed), 212kg (dry)

Sports-tourer bikes have really come into their own in recent years. Not so long ago, manufacturers used to apply this tag to sports models that had been superseded by their own latest highly-advanced offerings, rounding their harder edges and repackaging them as fast but friendly comfortable all-rounders.

Nowadays, the manufacturers are wise to the needs of intrepid travellers who want the performance to take them where they want to go quickly, and the handling to let them exploit the most exciting route there. Of course, there's nothing to stop you touring on a regular sportsbike, and many people see hypersports bikes (see previous page) as good choices. But if you're planning to take a pillion, most sportsbikes are going to be pretty uncomfortable for them even before the first fuel stop, which will come round a lot quicker than on a sports-tourer with its (usually) greater tank range.

The bike that defined the sports-tourer class is Honda's VFR800, a V4 that started life as a 750. For some years it has featured the company's VTEC variable valve system. Standard anti-lock braking makes for an even more refined package. Other Hondas you might look at are the NT700V Deauville, CBF1000 and, of course, the STX1300 Pan European.

Where Honda led, others followed, overtaking even the VFR in some areas of performance. A good example is Triumph's Sprint ST, which features the 1050cc motor also found in the Speed Triple naked bike.

By definition, any sports-tourer is something of a compromise – there are better sportsbikes and there are better tourers. Don't get too hung up on spurious definitions. Look at rider and pillion comfort first, luggage capacity and tank range second. Speed, handling, and space are the key definitions of what makes a great sports tourer. And don't be constrained by where a bike hails from.

If European twins are your thing, you might also like to look at Aprilia's Falco V-twins and BMW's R1200ST shaft-drive boxer.

Because their performance is down on their full-on sports brethren's, and insurers perceive them as tending to attract more 'sensible' riders, sports-tourers fall into similar insurance groups to 600cc sportsbikes, although they mostly cost a bit more to buy. But if you weigh up the price of buying close to big-bore sportsbike performance against lower premiums, sports-tourers start to look like very good value indeed.

Tourers

In theory you can tour on any bike you like, just as, in theory, you can cross the Atlantic in a canoe. But if your aspirations are more club class than leaky coracle, you'll be wanting a full-blown tourer for your high-mileage excursions.

BMW K1200LT in-line 4-cylinder 16-valve, 1171cc, 98bhp (claimed), 378kg (dry)

Honda's Gold Wing represents the pinnacle of grand touring. In its current incarnation, the Wing boasts a huge 1832cc, flat six-cylinder, fuel-injected motor pumping out a claimed 123ft-lb of torque at a lowly 4000rpm – more than enough to push along its 363kg. A massive 25-litre fuel tank allows you to cover the length of small countries between fuel stops. Just activate the cruise control, sit back and enjoy the ride. An optional six-CD autochanger provides the entertainment on the more boring stretches, or you can talk to your pillion in their armchair-like seat over the intercom. Feeling the windblast? Simply adjust the screen or combat the chill by opening the heater vents, which divert warm air from the engine towards the rider.

There's plenty of room in the lockable panniers – nearly 150 litres – to stash holiday souvenirs and the duty-frees.

The Wing's bulk makes it difficult to carve through traffic like you can on other bikes, but it's otherwise surprisingly nimble for its size. There's even a reverse gear, should you find the need.

Looking at the Wing now, it's hard to believe that it was originally conceived as a sportsbike. But that was back in the late 1970s, when big-cubed motors were seen as the only way to go for performance. Honda soon wised up and the Wing went down another evolutionary path.

If the Wing's opulence seems a little over the top, then there are plenty of other, less-imposing tourers available, but some are almost as well appointed, such as BMW's K1200LT.

Sportsbike purists may scoff at the big tourers, arguing that they have all the disadvantages of a car with none of the advantages of a bike. But with excellent weather protection and superior comfort, maybe the tourists are having the last laugh. In any case, they can't hear you above their CD players.

Taking a peek under the skin of Honda's mighty GL1800 Gold Wing. Big everything. Luxurious seating (bottom left), note speakers and intercom jack. 'What does this button do, dad?' (centre). Should just about hold the duty-free haul (bottom right). Be sure to check for stowaways.

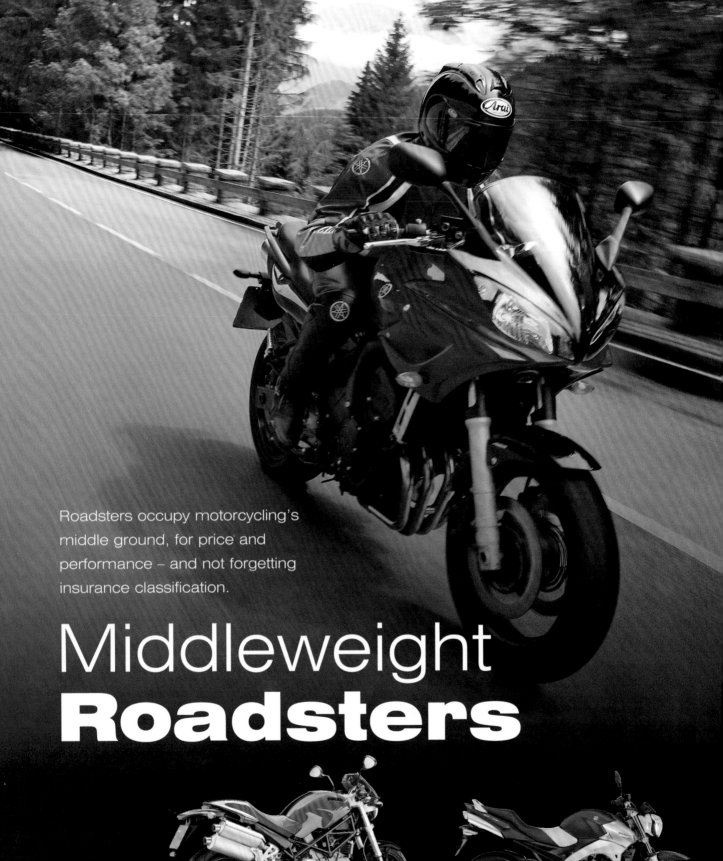

Roadsters occupy motorcycling's middle ground, for price and performance – and not forgetting insurance classification.

Middleweight
Roadsters

Ducati Monster S2R air-cooled V-twin, 4-valve, 803cc, 76bhp (claimed), 173kg (dry)

Suzuki GSR600 in-line 4-cylinder 16-valve, 599cc, 98bhp (claimed), 183kg (dry)

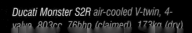

Honda Hornet 600
in-line 4-cylinder 16-valve, 599cc, 95bhp (claimed), 178kg (dry)

Bikes such as the Yamaha Fazer, Honda Hornet and Suzuki Bandit 600 are ideal first choices for riders who have recently passed their tests. Their user-friendly riding positions and power delivery make for a package that won't intimidate less experienced riders, or rush them headlong into trouble.

Bikes in this class make great all-rounders, even if they don't excel at anything in particular – apart from providing relatively cheap fun.

They lack sportsbike levels of ground clearance, so crazy lean angles are out. But there's enough there for you to cut your trackday teeth on, should you choose. Bikes such as the Fazer and Hornet 600s have detuned engines from earlier Yamaha and Honda sportsbikes. They might lack the top-end of the original sportsbike incarnations but the engines have plenty of mid-range for punchy acceleration. Wind and weather protection is minimal on roadsters since they are usually unfaired – although some have nose cones or half fairings – so they wouldn't be first choice for touring.

Honda also have the CBF600 ABS, available with and without anti-lock brakes and an optional half fairing.

Roadsters are built using conventional components, and this is reflected in their cost. Frames are usually cheap tubular steel, not the aluminium alloy spars of sportsbikes. Suspension is usually functional, but budget and non-adjustable. But, pound for pound, roadsters represent great fun.

At the less sparkling end of the performance spectrum lie bikes such as the Honda CB500 ABS and Kawasaki ER5 twins, the latter recently joined by the 650cc ER-6N and the faired ER-6F. Kawasaki's lusty Z750 provides an option in the 750 four-cylinder roadster class. The Fazer 600 and Hornet 600 offer performance that in the right hands can worry sportsbikes.

If you want something different, go for the Italian Cagiva Raptor 650 or the Suzuki SV650, both of which use a 645cc V-twin engine from the Japanese company. And there are Ducati's 618 and 803cc V-twin Monsters.

So even if a roadster can't give you a total sportsbike buzz, the money you'll save on insurance, servicing and consumables provides plenty of compensation.

Kawasaki ER-5 *parallel twin-cylinder 8-valve, 498cc, 50bhp (claimed), 179kg (dry)*

Suzuki SV650 *liquid-cooled V-twin-cylinder 8-valve, 645cc, 70bhp (claimed), 165kg (dry)*

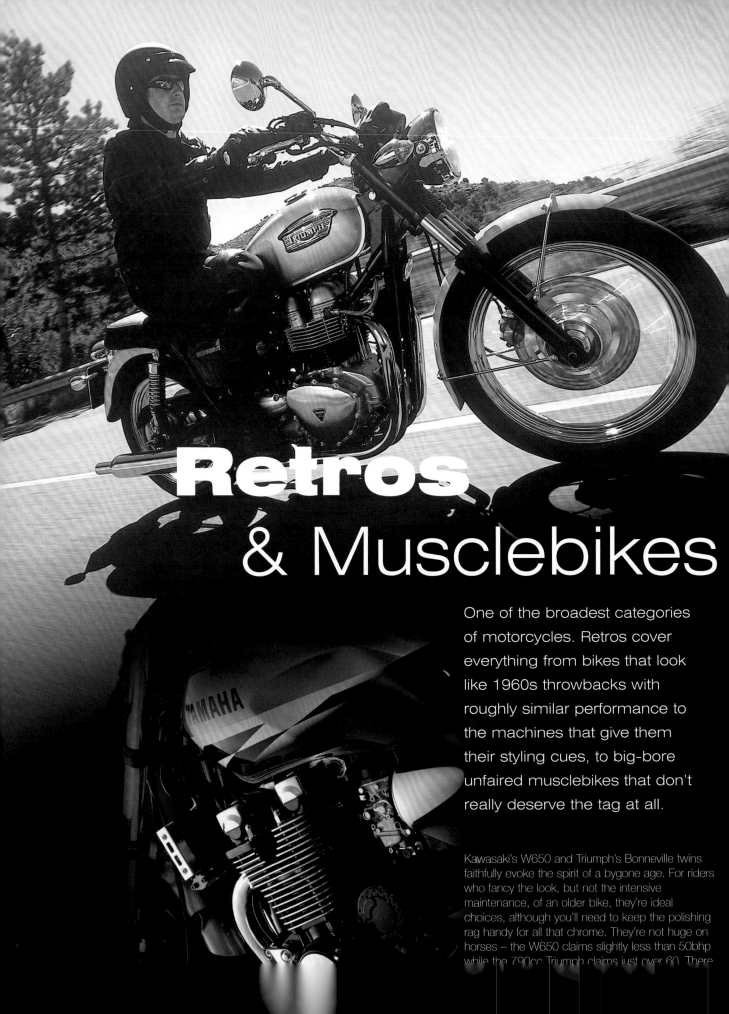

Retros
& Musclebikes

One of the broadest categories of motorcycles. Retros cover everything from bikes that look like 1960s throwbacks with roughly similar performance to the machines that give them their styling cues, to big-bore unfaired musclebikes that don't really deserve the tag at all.

Kawasaki's W650 and Triumph's Bonneville twins faithfully evoke the spirit of a bygone age. For riders who fancy the look, but not the intensive maintenance, of an older bike, they're ideal choices, although you'll need to keep the polishing rag handy for all that chrome. They're not huge on horses – the W650 claims slightly less than 50bhp while the 790cc Triumph claims just over 60. There is a more powerful 865cc Thruxton version claiming 69bhp. The real back wheel figures will be close to those of the 1960s bikes they mimic. Overhead camshafts and electric starters will be unfamiliar to those who remember pushrod engines and kickstarts, twinshock rear suspension lives on in a world where the monoshock is the new standard. Same goes for the air rather than liquid cooling of the engines. And, of course, owners of these modern classics can enjoy the image with the reassurance that their bikes have 21st century brakes and reliability.

At the other end of the scale sit big-bore naked bikes such as Yamaha's XJR1300 and Suzuki's GSX1400, whose commanding presence makes them look meaner than they really are.

Another Suzuki, the 1200 Bandit, is a cult in its own right, with a motor derived from the company's legendary, bullet-proof GSX-R1100. For many years the Bandit 12 was the naked hooligan weapon of choice, but it's been made ever softer by Suzuki and now the early bikes are the ones to have.

Yamaha's Fazer 1000 has a detuned motor from the R1 sportsbike – less top-end but loads in the middle. And where it beats its contemporaries, apart from performance, is in its handling. Where other bikes in the class tend to offer big motors in budget chassis, the Yam skimps in neither department – but that is reflected in the list price. There's the FZ1 too, but glitchy fuelling hasn't earned the bike too many devotees despite its use of a recent R1 motor.

Honda followed the big Fazer into the fray with the Hornet 900. Its chassis is less well appointed than the Yam's, but it is cheaper and uses an engine from an earlier FireBlade, again detuned to take some off the top and boost the middle. To rival the big Yam they have the CBF1000, with optional ABS.

If you want a V-twin in the big naked class look at Cagiva's Suzuki TL1000-engined Raptors. Ducati's big Monsters are rightly popular too, and now they also offer the Sport Classic models, although these are bulbous, crude editions of the bikes from which they drew their inspiration.

Retros, nakeds – call them what you will – are huge fun. They're cheaper to insure than the latest cutting-edge sportsbikes, but will give you plenty to grin about.

Suzuki GSX1400 in-line 4-cylinder 16-valve, 1402cc, 104bhp (claimed), 228kg (dry)

Yamaha FZ1 Fazer in-line 4-cylinder 20-valve, 998cc, 150bhp (claimed), 199kg (dry)

Kawasaki W650 parallel twin-cylinder 8-valve, 676cc, 49.6bhp (claimed), 195kg (dry)

Kawasaki ZRX1200R in-line 4-cylinder 16-valve, 1164cc, 120bhp (claimed), 223kg (dry)

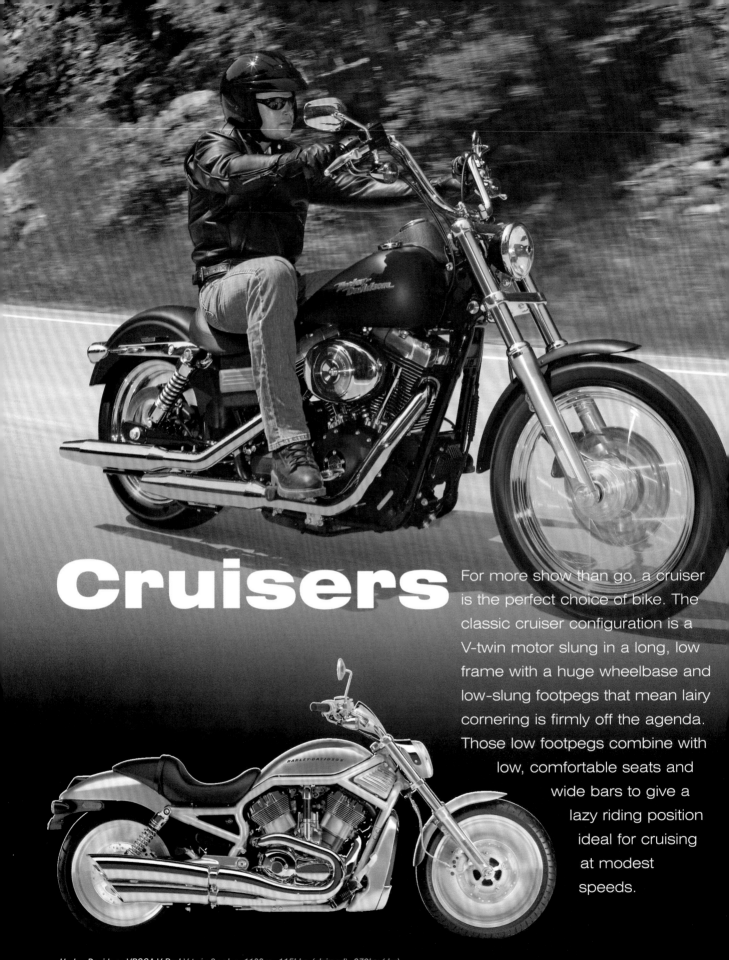

Cruisers

For more show than go, a cruiser is the perfect choice of bike. The classic cruiser configuration is a V-twin motor slung in a long, low frame with a huge wheelbase and low-slung footpegs that mean lairy cornering is firmly off the agenda. Those low footpegs combine with low, comfortable seats and wide bars to give a lazy riding position ideal for cruising at modest speeds.

Harley-Davidson VRSCA V-Rod V-twin 8-valve, 1130cc, 115bhp (claimed), 279kg (dry)

Suzuki VL1500LC Intruder V-twin 6-valve, 1462cc, 66bhp (claimed), 292kg (dry)

Yamaha Dragstar 650 V-twin 4-valve, 649cc, 39bhp (claimed), 229kg (dry)

Kawasaki VN1600 Mean Streak V-twin 8-valve, 1552cc, 72bhp (claimed), 290kg (dry)

Love 'em or loathe 'em, there is no class of bike more likely to provoke extreme devotion or extreme derision than cruisers. So just sit back and enjoy the scenery and the easy riding of motorcycling's showiest showboats.

Harley-Davidsons epitomise the cruiser style, and for many purists anything else is a feeble imitation. But these days most manufacturers offer a cruiser based on the famous Harley lines. Most feature V-twin motors in a lowly state of tune, designed to deliver optimum torque from minimal revs. They come in all sizes from all sorts of manufacturers, from Honda's 125cc Shadow to Yamaha's mammoth XV1900 Midnight Star. Despite its massive displacement, the Midnight Star claims just 100bhp. But big cruisers are all about torque for lowdown and mid-range drive.

One exception to the V-twin cruiser rule is Triumph's Rocket III, a 2294cc beast with an inline three-cylinder motor that can punt the bike's huge 320kg bulk to 60mph faster than virtually any other standard bike. Again it's all about torque, which the Rocket has in spades.

Moto Guzzi has various V-twin cruiser alternatives, but this time the cylinders are arranged across the frame rather than in line with it.

Most cruisers boast enough chrome to keep even the most avid of polishers happy, and if your bike of choice doesn't have quite enough shiny bits for you, there is an endless array of aftermarket bolt-ons to let you customise your steed. If that still doesn't make it sufficiently eye-catching, you can always fit some slash-cut straight-through pipes to herald your arrival.

You get plenty of metal for your money with cruisers, and most are as heavy as their performance is ponderous.

Harley look-alikes became popular because they were often more refined than the Milwaukee vibrators from which they unashamedly stole their looks. Liquid-cooled engines, overhead camshafts and shaft drive were niceties not to be found on the more traditional Harleys, whose harder edges play a big part in their appeal to devotees. But maybe things have come full circle with the Harley V-Rod, a liquid-cooled, double overhead cam, eight-valve V-twin that can haul its 279kg self up the standing quarter mile in 11.5 seconds. Purists will be pleased to hear that the long wheelbase, low seat, wide bars and forward pegs are still present and correct. But what to call the thing. A sports cruiser?

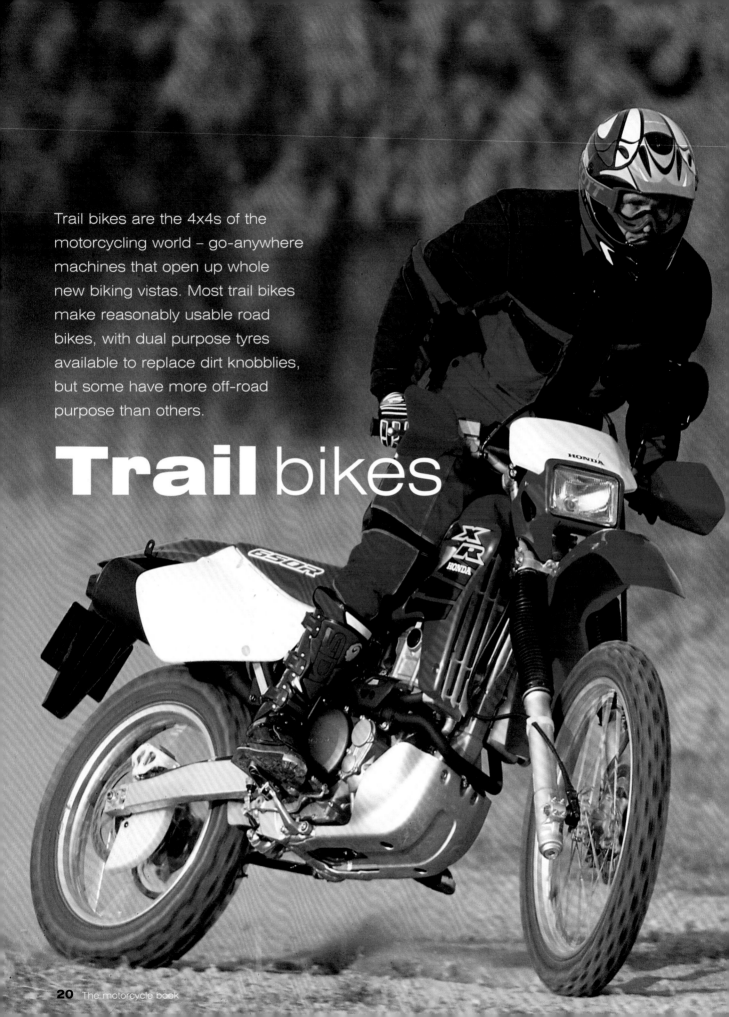

Trail bikes are the 4x4s of the motorcycling world – go-anywhere machines that open up whole new biking vistas. Most trail bikes make reasonably usable road bikes, with dual purpose tyres available to replace dirt knobblies, but some have more off-road purpose than others.

Trail bikes

Suzuki DRZ400 single-cylinder 4-valve, 398cc, 39bhp (claimed), 132kg (dry)

Trail bikes used to be all about the light weight and simplicity of a two-stroke – but the legislators have seen most of these off as dual-purpose road and off-road bikes; they simply couldn't meet the emissions regulations.

Four-strokes are heavier but tend to offer more longevity than a stroker – Honda's XLR125 and Suzuki's DR125 are top choices here.

Going up a bit in capacity, Suzuki's DR-Z400S four-stroke has proved popular since its introduction in 2000. It replaced the DR350, a favourite of clubman enduro event off-road riders, and packs a torquey 398cc motor in a compact, motocross-style chassis. An ideal choice for the trails.

Specialist manufacturers such as Beta, Gas Gas, Husqvarna, and KTM bring years of off-road market experience to bear on their dirtbikes.

Beta is renowned for its trial's competition (as distinct from trail) bikes, and its Alps – available in 200 and 350cc versions with Suzuki engines – are four-stroke bikes that draw on that trial's heritage while offering more general purpose utility.

Gas Gas offer a range of enduro and trail bikes from 49 to 300cc in two-stroke form as well as a 450cc four-stroke.

The Husqvarna WRE125 is a gorgeous little two-stroke that also happens to be learner-legal and available in supermoto form too. And the company's TE450, 510 and 610 are big four-stroke thumpers for dedicated trail riders, again available in supermoto trim.

KTM has an excellent choice of off-roaders for the trail rider, from 250cc two-strokes to 625cc four-strokes.

Trail riding is an excellent way to discover old byways that have escaped the scourge of tarmac, but bridleways and footpaths are off-limits in the UK. Because the trails are legally highways, your bike must be road-legal, including MoT and insurance. Show other trail users such as walkers and horse riders courtesy and respect the countryside. That way, trail riding will continue to be one of the great outdoor pursuits.

Honda's XR650 (facing page) gives plenty of four-stroke grunt and torque without imposing too big a weight penalty on the trail rider. Still, looks like this bloke's having fun, and that's what trail riding's all about. As dirty as you can get with your clothes on.

Legislation has killed off new two-stroke trailies like the Kawasaki KDX125 – still a good second-hand buy.

Honda XLR125R single-cylinder 2-valve, 124.1cc, 11.4bhp (claimed), 119kg (dry)

Honda XL1000V Varadero V-twin 8-valve, 999cc, 95bhp (claimed), 220kg (dry)

Honda XL650V Transalp V-twin 6-valve, 647cc, 54.3bhp (claimed), 191kg (dry)

Monster trailies

They might take their styling cues from off-roaders, but most monster trailies aren't really for the rough stuff unless you have the strength and abilities of a Paris–Dakar desert racing hero.

BMW R1200GS flat twin 8-valve, 1170cc, 100bhp (claimed), 199kg (dry)

Despite their looks, monster trailies excel best on the road, especially in town. High riding position and wide bars make for a great view of the road and easy steering. Big-bore engines display a huge appetite for munching the miles. And huge fuel tanks extend the range between filling stations. But while the soft suspension delivers a comfortable ride, it also means cornering potential isn't in the sportsbike league, and that upright riding position puts you right in the windblast. Still, if sportsbikes aren't your bag, a big trailie might be the thing.

Aprilia's Capo Nord is a good example of a monster trailie. With a 997cc V-twin engine taken from Aprilia's sportier big twins (detuned to make less than 100bhp) the Capo Nord is a big softie that also has a harder edge when you turn it up a bit. A tall screen takes away the worst of the wind.

Cagiva's Navigator offers a similar package, its V-twin engine taken from Suzuki's TL1000. BMW's flat twin R1200GS is the largest and latest of over two decades' worth of big Bee-Em trailies. GS

stands for Gelande/Strasse, which translates roughly into English as off-road/road, so you can see where the regular Paris–Dakar winning firm is coming from.

Other options include Honda's Varadero, powered by the one-litre V-twin lump from the Firestorm sportsbike. Triumph's 955cc Tiger triple is popular too, as is Yamaha's TDM900 twin.

KTM rocked the class to its foundations with the launch of their 990 Adventure and Superduke. As BMW's main Dakar rivals, they're also taking on the Germans in the road bike class too.

If the trail bike style is your thing but you need less than a litre in the engine department, look at bikes such as the BMW F650GS single – a 50bhp four-stroke. Honda's Transalp is a 647cc alternative and the KTM 640 Adventure is another top choice. Suzuki have the DL650 V-Strom too.

Big trailies are extremely popular in continental Europe, and make sound sense as capable all-rounders.

Monster trailies are imposing machines. You can make an aggressive Paris–Dakar statement on the road, even if your off-road ambitions extend no further than bumping on to the pavement outside the cafe.

Suzuki V-Strom V-twin 8-valve, 996cc, 98bhp (claimed), 211kg (dry)

Aprilia Capo Nord V-twin 8-valve, 997.6cc, 98bhp (claimed), 215kg (dry)

Supermotos

Supermotos are the new kids on the biking block and have enjoyed a huge upsurge in interest over the past decade. Supermoto racing is huge in continental Europe and is fast gaining a foothold in the UK, although its origins can be traced back to the 1970s in the States.

KTM Duke single-cylinder, 4-valve, 625cc, 55bhp (claimed), 145kg (dry)

Yamaha XT660R single-cylinder, liquid-cooled, 659cc, 44bhp (claimed), 165kg (dry).
Mainstream Japanese take on the supermoto theme. Too slow and heavy for serious off-road work.

When you buy most supermotos, you essentially get a race bike with the legal niceties of lights, indicators and a speedo tacked on. Usually big four-stroke singles, supermotos are being marketed to road riders as fun alternatives to sportsbikes for those riders who don't trust themselves to stick to licence-conserving speeds. And there's something in that. Big, torquey motors and low gearing make them a blast off the line, and if wheelies light your fire, a supermoto will more than happily oblige. Dynamite brakes and light weight make stoppies a breeze too. And top speeds rarely exceed 100mph, keeping licences safe. On the other hand, high riding positions and big, thumping single cylinders aren't much fun on long straights, and small fuel tanks limit mileage between refills.

However, invest in a spare set of wheels for off-road tyres and you have two bikes for the price of one (plus a set of wheels, of course). Most supermotos come with trick, high-quality, off-road suspension, which is more than adequate on the road.

European companies dominate the supermoto market. British firm CCM get their power from Suzuki single engines. They build stripped-down competition derived machines, as well as slightly more refined offerings with larger fuel tanks for more road-going versatility.

Austrian firm KTM is another big name in supermotos, thanks to plenty of competition success. The KTM 640 Duke is a 625cc four-stroke single and production is limited to 1500 bikes per year. There's also the 660 SMC supermoto, which boasts a bored out version of the same engine but more basic off-road styling. Italian firm Husqvarna (formed originally in Sweden) has the 576cc four-stroke 610 SM, introduced as the supermoto version of its TE610 enduro bike. Husky also offers the SM510R – more of a hardcore performer, which like all supermotos has a very high seat.

Japanese offerings are the more refined Honda FMX650 and Yamaha XT660X, which don't really appeal to the hardcore supermotard.

Supermotos are plenty of fun. Putting a big off-roader on 17-inch road wheels with sticky rubber is a sure-fire recipe for loads of laughs. Just stay away from the straights.

Supermotos are useful in the inner city for carve-up merchants looking for something with more presence, punch, and cred than a scooter to haul them to work and back.

Supermotos started as a cult that is now gaining huge momentum. Initially the preserve of specialist manufacturers, it didn't take long for the large bike companies to move in on the action.

Commuters

Any motorcycle can be used as a commuter bike, but some are more suited than others. Riding a sportsbike, say, through the cut and thrust of an urban rush hour can be a regal pain in the neck and wrists, apart from the fact that those bikes are geared for far longer-legged riding. A scooter is a great choice provided your ride to work is over mainly low-speed roads. But lightweights and middleweights are the best overall.

Honda CBF500ABS parallel twin 8-valve, 499cc, 57bhp (claimed), 175kg (dry)

Honda CB600F Hornet in-line 4-cylinder 16-valve, 599cc, 95bhp (claimed), 178kg (dry)

There are two simple reasons that make an unfaired lightweight or middleweight – rather than a scooter – the top choice of commuter bike. Firstly, they're less likely to attract the attention of thieves when parked up outside work all day. And secondly, if you do come a cropper in the free-for-all that is modern town riding, the bike is likely to sustain minimal damage. Even the lightest tumble on a faired sportsbike is likely to result in a hefty bill because of the costly panels that make up the fairing.

The best alternatives to a bus pass or train season ticket are capable middleweights such as the Kawasaki ER-5 and Honda CBF500. Yamaha Fazer and Honda Hornet 600s also make good choices, and now there are the Kawasaki ER-6 and

Honda CBF600 ABS too, although they're a little more conspicuous than their blander brethren.

Suzuki offer plenty of options for the two-wheeled commuter, including the cheap and cheerful GS500 and faired GS500F parallel twins. Then there's the SV650 which is also available with a half fairing, the GSR600 inline four, and the ever popular Bandits.

Yamaha's MT-03 660cc single would brighten up the workaday commute too.

There are plenty of bikes capable of playing the commuter role, offering an undemanding ride and low maintenance. Just as important, they provide an economic alternative to other means of commuting. And that has to be reason enough to rip up your rail card and extend your motorcycling enjoyment to the everyday task of getting to work and back.

Look at this. BMW's F650 uses a dummy tank to make it the largest capacity, ride-to-work handbag on the planet. Add to that a belt final drive and it has to be a top choice for commuters who prefer to keep bike maintenance to a minimum.

Suzuki GS500E *parallel twin, 487cc, 51.3bhp (claimed), 173kg (dry)*

Yamaha MT-03 *single-cylinder, 660cc, 45bhp (claimed), 174kg (dry)*

Learner bikes

Unless you're going for a moped licence, at least some of your training will be done on a 125cc bike. And unless you're doing Direct or Accelerated Access (see page 39), you'll probably take your test on a 125 too.

Aprilia RS125R two-stroke single, 124.6cc, 12bhp (restricted), 115kg (dry)

Honda CLR125 City Fly single-cylinder 4-valve, 124.7cc, 15bhp (claimed) 145kg (dry)

Honda CG125 single-cylinder 4-valve, 124cc, 10.8bhp (claimed), 137kg (dry)

Honda's CG125 has established itself as a training school staple, and it's easy to see why. The bullet-proof little four-stroke single can take as much punishment as even the most novice learner can throw at it, and being a 125 it's economical too. Sure, it isn't exactly the most attractive bike on the planet, but it's more than capable enough for learning on and makes a useful commuter bike once you've passed your test. The front drum brake is a dated touch and not as powerful as a disc, but it's enough to pull up the CG.

You can, of course, learn on a school bike, but if you want your own and the CG125 lacks the street-cred you desire, there are loads of other 125s that mimic the styles of various bigger bikes. Honda offers a 125 custom (VT125 Shadow); the trail-style CLR125 City Fly; a proper trailie in the form of the XR125L; the sporty CBR125; and a baby monster trailie, the V-twin 125 Varadero.

Yamaha has the two-stroke DT125R and the four-stroke XT125R trailies, both available styled as supermotos too, and the YBR125 roadster.

Suzuki options extend to the four-stroke GZ125 Marauder and VL125 Intruder, the former a budget version of the latter and the balloon-tyred RV125 Vanvan.

Kawasaki provide the custom EL125 Eliminator. Off-road specialist Husqvarna offers a couple of 125s – the road-wheeled SM125S and knobbly-tyred WRE125 – but peaky power delivery and uncompromising off-road competition suspension make them perhaps not the best choice for novices.

Fancy a 125cc sportsbike? Aprilia's RS125 is a gorgeous two-stroke racer replica that looks and performs the part. They have the MX125 trailie/supermoto too.

Cagiva's Mito 125 looks like a baby Ducati 996, with a chassis capable of outhandling its two-stroke motor in restricted form. The company also offers the Raptor 125 naked.

There's plenty of choice in the 125 market and, just as important, something to suit most budgets.

Reflect your post-test bike aspirations in your choice of 125 for your learner days. Sports, custom, cruiser, trailie or roadster – they're all there in the eighth-of-a-litre class.

Suzuki GZ125 single cylinder, 2-valve, 124cc, 12bhp (claimed), 125kg (dry)

Honda XR125L single cylinder, 125cc, 11bhp (restricted), 109kg (dry)

Yamaha SR125 single-cylinder 2-valve, 124cc, 12bhp (claimed), 104kg (dry)

Classic bikes

If the latest tackle doesn't light your wick, what about a classic? People are drawn to classics for different reasons. Some older riders choose the bikes they either owned in their youth or couldn't afford back then. Other people just want to own and ride a legendary make or model. The simple satisfaction of keeping an old machine on the road can be a draw, too. And then there are the restorers, who buy machines to return them to original factory condition – known as concours – to show or to ride.

Given that bikes have been around for more than a century, there's plenty of choice. A pre-First World War single with a leather drive belt and only one gear might not make the best choice of ride-to-work bike in the 21st century. So if you plan to use your classic bike fairly frequently, go for something more recent – especially if you're looking at your first classic. It will be easier to source spares, particularly if your classic was a popular model, because for many of these, spares are being remanufactured, often improving on the original components.

By going for a classic, you're turning your back on at least two decades of machine development. For regular use, choose a classic with enough performance to keep pace with modern traffic, and remember that braking and reliability will not be as good as with modern machinery. Even so, there are a number of specialists supplying conversions to uprate brakes, replace points with electronic ignition, and generally make classics perform better and more reliably.

A huge network of classic enthusiasts' and owners' clubs exists to help keep older machinery on the road, so join a club relevant to your classic. Clubs are an indispensable source of advice and many run spares schemes, even going as far as remanufacturing parts if enough owners commit to buying them. They also organise runs and rallies, and many have regular local meetings, which are excellent opportunities to socialise with like-minded enthusiasts.

For many classic fans, the challenge of keeping their bikes on the road and the extra maintenance they tend to demand is all part of the fun – and most older bikes are far easier to work on than modern bikes, which is probably just as well.

As an added incentive, insurance for classics (normally defined as a bike built before 1984) is extremely cheap, but you'll have to hunt around for cover if you're under 25. And bikes built before 1 January 1973 are exempt from UK road tax. So you'll have a bit more cash for spare parts and consumables.

There are endless classics to choose from, but ideal selections for those new to the joys of older machines of character are the more common recent bikes for ease of spares availability and, in the case of bigger bikes, usable performance.

1973 Norton 750 Commando
parallel twin OHV, 748cc, 180kg (dry approx)

1981 Laverda Formula Mirage
inline triple DOHC, 1116cc, 232kg (dry)

Late Sixties Triumph Bonneville
parallel twin OHV, 649cc, 175kg (dry approx)

Scooters

The scooter market has been motorcycling's biggest boom area in the past few years, but it's more than a passing fad. Scooters offer a cheap and convenient alternative to a car – or even a bus pass. Fashion has played its part in the scooter's rise, but low running costs and cheap insurance are the real clinchers. Small, light and easy to park, scooters are the ultimate solution for battling through the urban jungle. Add in fuel consumption that redefines 'frugal' – 65mpg is the average, and some will happily do close to 100mpg – and scooters are a compelling option.

Aprilia Scarabeo
single-cylinder two stroke,
100/125cc, 92/140kg (dry)

Scooters are a tempting option for many reasons, including their ease of riding. Many are fully automatic – just twist the throttle and go. Most have enough storage space under the seat to store your helmet when you park up, and accommodate a generous load of shopping for the ride home.

It's fitting that scooters are again finding their place transporting urban commuters and riders, because that's how they originally came into being. After the Second World War, there was a huge need for cheap transport in Italy. Aeroplane factories were banned from making planes, but they still had the steel pressing machinery and a surplus of small wheels from making fighters. Out of this adversity, the original Vespa ('wasp') was born, and Italy got on the road again.

Many of today's most desirable scooters are Italian – Piaggio, Vespa, Aprilia. The French are big players too, in the form of Peugeot. And, of course, the Japanese manufacturers would never miss a market. So there's plenty of choice in this very competitive arena.

Suzuki, Yamaha, and Honda have been particularly active in creating a new class of superscooter and the Italians are getting in on the act too. These machines combine scooter levels of comfort and weather protection with top speeds (about 100mph) that allow them to keep up with motorway traffic.

But are these scooters or are they bikes? Honda has its 582cc SilverWing, Piaggio the X9 500, Suzuki the Burgman 400 and 650, while Yamaha offer the 500 TMax. There comes a point when the slimline attributes of the smaller scooters are compromised by the manufacturers' desire to be all things to all people.

Italjet Torpedo (above)
Scooter manufacturers are more than happy to tilt their hats to their heritage with swoopy lines and classic styling, while incorporating modern niceties such as disc brakes and indicators.

Italjet Dragster single-cylinder two-stroke, 50/125/180cc, 85/107/109kg (dry)

Honda @125 single-cylinder four-stroke, 13bhp (claimed), 120kg (dry)

Suzuki Burgman single-cylinder 4-valve, 385cc, 32bhp (claimed), 174kg (dry)

Mopeds

Not so long ago it was every 16-year-old's dream to own a moped, and the little fifties introduced many riders to a lifetime of motorcycling. Now the scooter boom has revived interest in motorcycling's mini marvels.

Honda SH50 City Express single cylinder two-stroke, 49cc, 3.8bhp (claimed), 68kg (dry)

Light weight and ease of operation characterise mopeds. At 16 years' old, they're your only powered two-wheeled option. Enjoy. More speed and power is only a year's riding away.

Aprilia SR50 Di Tech Racing
single-cylinder two-stroke, 50cc, 89kg (dry)

A moped is still the only way for anyone under 17 to use a powered machine on the road legally, and opens up a whole new world of freedom. Okay, there are limits. Top speed is limited to 30mph, maximum weight is 250kg (easy for a small two-wheeler to comply with) and maximum engine size is 50cc.

But while they might not be big on speed and power, they don't have to be small on style. The fashionable sixteener these days has plenty of choice.

Top scooter-style options include Aprilia's SR50LC sports moped and the Rally LC trail-style scooter moped. Scooters are huge in Italy and other Italian companies such as Benelli, Beta, Gilera, Italjet, Malaguti, MBK, Piaggio and, of course, Vespa have some stylish scootermopeds too – as do Spanish firm Derbi.

France isn't known as a big producer of bikes, but Peugeot's 50cc Speedfight has been a soaraway sales success largely because of its styling and handling.

The Japanese ignore few markets, and scooter-mopeds are no exception. Honda, Suzuki and Yamaha all offer scooter-style fifties.

If you're limited to moped performance but demand sportsbike looks, consider Aprilia's RS50, the Moto-Roma RX50, or the more powerful Derbi GPR50R – and head straight to the top of the school bike shed style charts.

There are plenty of trail-style, enduro and supermoto mopeds to choose from. Take your pick from the Aprilia RX50, Derbi Senda R, Gilera RCR50, and Sherco Supermoto 50 among others.

Mopeds are fun and economical, if lacking in power. A lot of mopeds are restricted, so the potential for more power is there. However, this can put the bike outside the scope of your licence – assuming the powers that be find out – and affect warranties and insurance cover. Many are twist-and-go automatics, particularly the scooter type, while others feature big-bike controls. Either way, they're a great introduction to the joys of biking.

Suzuki AP50W single-cylinder two-stroke, 49cc, 2.9bhp (claimed), 59kg (dry)

Aprilia Enjoy Racing electric bicycle, 31kg

2 Getting on the road

Which
test
option?

Having decided you want to go
motorcycling, you need to sort out
a licence before taking to the road.
Current UK legislation provides a
tiered route to motorcycle licences.
Which path you take depends on
your age and the type of bikes
you want your licence to cover –

Cut your riding teeth on a blue funky moped . . .

. . . then move up to the giddy power of a CG125

MOPEDS

Aspring riders aged 16 and older can apply for a moped licence. A moped is defined as a bike with a maximum design speed not exceeding 30mph, a weight of less than 250kg, an engine of 50cc or less, and capable of being propelled by pedals if it was first used before 1 September 1977. Hardly a heady mix, but the only option for 16 year-olds – and better than the bus. You'll have to apply for a provisional licence and take Compulsory Basic Training (see page 40) before being able to ride on the road with L-plates. Next, you'll have to pass the theory test (page 42) before taking the moped test. Pass that and you can rip up the L-plates, then get out on the road, carrying a pillion if you wish.

Holders of full car licences first issued before 1 February 2001 can ride a moped without L-plates and without the need to take CBT. If you passed your car test after that date and want to ride a moped, you will need to do CBT.

MOTORCYCLES

Would-be motorcycle riders over 17 will first require provisional bike entitlement. Car licence holders automatically have provisional bike entitlement, but if you have no licence at all, you'll need to apply for a provisional bike licence. As of 1 February 2002, newly qualified car drivers without full motorcycle licences will need to pass CBT to validate their moped riding entitlement.

A provisional motorcycle licence entitles you to ride bikes under 125cc with a power output of no more than 14.6bhp, with L-plates, once you've passed your Compulsory Basic Training (page 40). You can't carry a pillion at this stage.

With CBT under your belt, it's time to take the theory test (page 42). Your CBT certificate and your theory test pass are valid for two years only and you'll have to retake both if you don't pass your full licence inside that time.

There are three types of motorcycle licence:
1 A1
2 Restricted Licence (A Licence)
3 Direct/Accelerated Access.

If your motorcycling ambition extends no further than a little 125 to get around on, then you'll want to go for an A1 licence. The route for this is the same as for a normal licence, but you'll take your

test on a bike of 75–125cc and thereafter be restricted to bikes under 125cc with a power output of no more than 14.6bhp.

The 'restricted' part of the Restricted Licence is the power of the bike you'll be allowed to ride for the two years after you've passed your test – no more than 33bhp or with a power-to-weight ratio under 0.21bhp/kg. Your training school will be able to provide you with a list of bikes that meet these criteria. It is also possible to have a more powerful machine modified to bring its power output in line with the law. In the meantime, you'll be learning on a bike with an engine of 120–125cc, a power output of 14.6bhp and capable of at least 100kmh (62mph in the old money). Training for a Restricted Licence obviously goes beyond the rudimentary skills you learned for the CBT. Riders of any age who want to start out on less powerful machines can opt for a Restricted Licence, but under-21s have no choice.

Younger riders can opt for Accelerated Access if they reach the age of 21 within the two-year restricted period after passing their test. This allows riders to move up to bikes of unlimited power by passing a further test on a bike of 46.6bhp or more. But while you are learning on the larger machine, it's back to L-plates accompanied by an instructor on the road – it's okay, he doesn't sit on the bike with you, he rides his own – but you're still free to ride your sub-33bhp bike unaccompanied.

Anyone over 21 years old can opt for Direct Access. This is the quickest route to a full bike licence, entitling the holder to ride a bike of any power. You'll take your CBT either on a learner bike or larger machine. Once you've passed that, you are allowed to ride a learner bike on the road with L-plates, but an instructor will have to accompany you on the larger bike, which must have a minimum output of 46.6bhp. Kawasaki ER-5s and Honda CB500s are popular choices of training schools.

Whichever training route you choose or are restricted to, you will be able to train and pass your test on bikes hired from your riding school. Many loan riding gear too. This means you can make the financial commitment to a bike and kit once you've passed your test and are sure that biking's for you. But if you want to practice in the meantime, you'll need your own kit and learner bike.

Aspiring riders line up to take the first steps to two-wheel freedom at a riding school (opposite). Everyone has to reach the same basic standard before passing their test.

Compulsory **B**asic **T**raining

Compulsory Basic Training means just what it says, but what does it involve? Its main purpose is to provide you with the fundamental skills for your own road safety as you embark on your biking career. CBT was devised to reduce the accident rate among young and novice riders, and statistics seem to show it's had a positive effect.

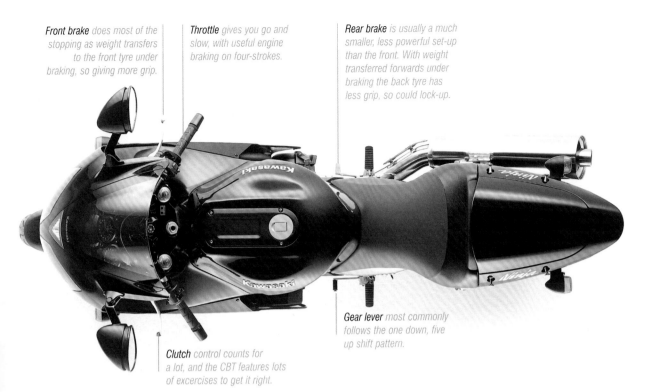

Front brake *does most of the stopping as weight transfers to the front tyre under braking, so giving more grip.*

Throttle *gives you go and slow, with useful engine braking on four-strokes.*

Rear brake *is usually a much smaller, less powerful set-up than the front. With weight transferred forwards under braking the back tyre has less grip, so could lock-up.*

Gear lever *most commonly follows the one down, five up shift pattern.*

Clutch *control counts for a lot, and the CBT features lots of excercises to get it right.*

You can take CBT on your own learner bike or moped, or else hire one from your training school (look in *Yellow Pages* for your local training organisations). If you don't have your own riding kit, then gloves, helmets and waterproofs can be hired or borrowed from most schools. Wear sturdy boots, a jacket (leather is best) and jeans in the absence of proper riding kit. The whole ensemble will be topped off by a fetching fluorescent bib provided by the school.

Remember to take your licence with you. The instructor will want to check it before training begins. The next formality is the eye test, where you'll be expected to read an ordinary car numberplate from 20.5 metres. If you usually wear glasses, you must wear them for this part of your CBT as well as the training and the eventual test.

By now, you'll be itching to get on with the business of riding, but first the classroom beckons for a look at what CBT involves and a chat about clothing and riding equipment. Then it's on to the training ground, where you'll be talked through the basics of what the bike's controls do, and practice getting the bike off and on its main stand.

At last it's time to get down to the riding itself. You'll master starting the bike, clutch control, pulling away, controlled braking and emergency stops, turning and U-turns. All this is done in the safe confines of the training ground, which is usually a piece of hard standing a bit like a car park, marked out with cones and white lines for the various exercises. Your instructor will ensure that you get all the tuition you need to grasp the various manouevres. Don't panic if things don't seem to be coming easily, because your instructor will give

you all the time and advice you need to crack it.

Just when you're bursting to get out on the road to practise your new-found skills, it's back to class for more instruction. This time you'll find out about riding and the law, the Highway Code, riding in traffic and anticipating other road users. You'll also learn that the need to take account of weather and road conditions is even more acute on a bike than it is in a car. It's all relevant stuff, even to learner riders who have been driving cars for years.

Next you'll put all the classroom theory and the hands-on work on the training ground into practice, with an accompanied road ride that lasts for at least two hours. You'll be equipped with a radio, on which you'll be told what to do by the instructor from his bike. You'll be working on road speed and positioning as you negotiate various junctions and roundabouts, observations (in front and behind), signalling, manoeuvring and more emergency stops. The route you ride is designed to take in most everyday hazards and situations you'll encounter out on the road.

Back at the training centre, provided the instructor's satisfied you've cracked it, you'll be issued with form DL196, your CBT pass. Now you're on the way to your full bike licence and are free to take to the road unaccompanied on a 125cc bike or moped with L-plates, depending on which licence you're aiming for.

CBT takes most riders a day, but don't be downhearted if it takes you longer. Everyone learns at different rates and, remember, your instructor wants to be sure that you're safe. A CBT certificate lasts for two years. If you don't pass your main test in that time, you'll have to take it again.

This learner is getting to grips with the basics of machine control. If he's doing Direct Access he could be on a bike like the 178bhp Kawasaki ZX-12R at the top of the page quite soon.

The **theory** test

With CBT under your belt, the next thing you'll need to pass is your theory test – and that includes holders of car licences too. The only learners exempt from this are moped riders, who obtained their licences by doing a two-part test.

To pass the theory test you'll need to provide 30 correct answers to 35 questions taken from a list of about 300. The questions relate to the meanings of road signs, and the techniques and theory of road safety. Various books containing sample questions have been published and the Driving Standards Agency publishes an official volume called *The Official Theory Test for Motorcyclists*. The whole process has been brought into the computer age too, with a CD-ROM available to help you learn your stuff.

You need to pass your theory test before proceeding to the main test, so do it as soon as you can. Remember that, like the CBT, a theory test pass expires after two years if you haven't passed your main test. If that happens, you'll have to resit it.

In addition to the theory test there is also a hazard perception test. This involves 14 one minute video clips that candidates have to respond to with actions such as change of speed or direction. The earlier a hazard is spotted, the higher the score. The test contains 15 scoreable hazards and there are five points available for each. Pass mark is 35 out of 75 for motorcycle riders.

The **main** test

Now you're ready for the big one. Time to put everything you've learned in your training under the scrutiny of a DSA examiner in a test lasting up to 40 minutes. Restricted licence candidates will take the test on a 125, but if you're going for a direct or accelerated licence you'll be doing it on a bike of over 46.6bhp.

Your instructor will have to accompany you to the test centre if you're sitting the test on the larger bike. Provided everything goes to plan, he won't be legally required to accompany you on the way back!

The examiner will want to check your documents – licence, CBT and theory test passes – and you'll need to have a signed photo ID with you. This last item is required to discourage candidates from sending someone else along to sit the test for them. You'll be asked to do the same eye test as in CBT (reading a car numberplate from 20.5 metres).

With the formalities out of the way, it's time to take to the road. You'll be kitted out with a two-way radio, like those used by the training school, so the examiner can give you instructions.

The examiner's looking for you to ride safely, sensibly and confidently, and there are certain things the test must cover, regardless of whether it lasts for the whole 40 minutes. You'll have practised all of these at training level. There'll be a separate hill start if the route doesn't feature a junction or set of lights on a hill, where you'd have to perform a hill start in the ordinary course of events. You'll also have to set off safely at an angle from behind a parked vehicle. There'll be an emergency stop, controlled and without locking up any wheels. You'll also have to do a U-turn and a slow ride with the examiner walking alongside, you matching his pace, to make sure your slow-machine control is up to scratch.

Provided you manage to do the set elements of the test competently, and don't make any dangerous or potentially dangerous mistakes on the rest of the ride, you'll pass and be able to rip up those L-plates. Congratulations.

You aren't allowed to take a passenger just yet, though. You have to wait until you've sent off your pass certificate and received your full licence.

Don't let your new-found two-wheel freedom go to your head. If you rack up six or more penalty points in your first two years of riding, you'll lose your licence and have to go through the theory and main tests again. As much as you've enjoyed learning to ride, you don't really want to do it all over again, do you?

Advanced
training

Advanced training has something to offer everyone – whether you've just passed your test, have been riding for years, or are returning to motorcycling after a break from it.

If the ink is barely dry on your bike licence, you might be wondering why you should want to have even more tuition. After all, you've just successfully taken on a whole load of new knowledge and shown the authorities that you know what you're doing, thank you very much. But steep though the learning curve was from wobbly-wheeled novice at CBT to confident, competent rider in the main test, there's always more to learn beyond the bare basics of control that you had to show the examiner. You can accelerate the process and become a faster and safer rider at the same time by taking some advanced training.

Or if you're coming back into motorcycling after a few years away, you can gain an instant boost to your confidence on today's faster bikes and busier road systems by signing up for extra tuition. Even riders who've been at it for years can benefit.

There are a huge number of advanced training organisations springing up, and there's a course to suit you whatever level of skills you currently have. At the moment, there is little formal regulation of advanced training organisations. That's not to say that every other school is a cowboy outfit, but be guided by the recommendations of other riders, bike magazines and dealers.

Many schools are run by ex-police riders and instructors, most of whom will be offering training based around the techniques in 'Roadcraft', the police riding manual. That doesn't mean they make their pupils bimble around in fluorescent jackets – you'll be making what they describe as 'good progress' outside 30, 40 and 50mph zones. But be assured you'll be making that 'good progress' at a rate you're comfortable with. A good instructor will be sensitive to the pace you want to learn and ride at, and will help you concentrate on the areas you most want to improve on. If the pupil-to-instructor ratio is more than one-to-one, a good school will also ensure that pupils of similar ability work with each instructor. That way, no one will be left behind by the rest of the group, and no one will feel held back by the group.

Central to advanced training is observation, and learning to make the most appropriate 'progress' you can in any set of circumstances. You'll hone your machine control techniques to corner and overtake faster and safer, and make the optimum use of your brakes. And the more all this stuff becomes second nature to you, the more fun you'll have on a bike.

Apart from the independent operators, the Institute of Advanced Motorcyclists offers economical advanced training in various parts of the country, as does the British Motorcyclists Federation. Your local police force may offer training too.

With proper instruction, you can learn techniques in a day or two, which otherwise might take years for you to develop on your own. And once you've learned advanced techniques you'll use them every time you ride. View every ride as an opportunity to hone your skills and technique.

Advanced training on the road (above) involves accompanied rides where experienced instructors assess your riding. The California Superbike School (left) holds track-based training in the UK too, where the emphasis is on developing machine control.

A student of the California Superbike School puts the theory into practice, developing skills on the track that will improve his road riding too. The right mix of road and track advanced training makes for more rounded and safer riders.

Think you're fast? Explore the limits of your bike and your riding ability by going on a trackday, or guarantee improved skills by signing up for a race school. And you'll be able to go out on challenging and famous circuits without making the huge commitments of time and cash demanded by racing.

Trackdays

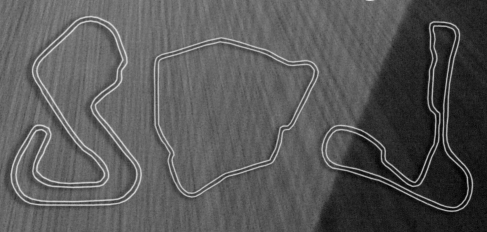

Brands Hatch   Castle Combe   Cadwell Park

Helmet *Most circuits will expect you to wear a lid with an ACU Gold Seal (below).*

Gloves *Choose race-style for adequate protection and good feel.*

Leathers *A good one-piece is best, a zip-together two-piece is the next choice.*

Knee sliders *Trackday heroics can be measured in how many pairs of sliders you get through. Most circuits frown on sparkies.*

Boots *Good race boots are best for protection and feel.*

The popularity of trackdays has led to a burgeoning industry that offers events countrywide pretty much all year round.

Apart from yourself and your bike, you'll need one-piece or good quality zip-together two-piece leathers (see page 50), a helmet with a gold ACU stamp (page 48), gloves (page 54) and boots (page 56). You may be required to tape up lights, indicators and mirrors. Most trackday organisers require you to show your driving licence when you sign on at an event, to prove that you've at least some idea of how to ride a bike. This is a condition imposed on them by their insurers. You'll be asked to fill out an indemnity form to limit the liability of the organisers, stating that you understand the nature of the event and that you're fit to take part. Don't forget to check with your own insurers that your policy extends to trackdays. If it doesn't, arrange additional cover, just in case the worst happens.

At most trackdays, riders are divided into groups depending on ability, ranging from novice (slow) to advanced (close to race pace). Choose the group you reckon you'll be most comfortable in. If you find yourself running rings round everyone in the slow group, then have the organisers move you up. It's better that way than starting out in too quick a group, being unsettled by faster riders rattling past you and having to haul yourself and your dented confidence down a class.

Before the track time begins, you'll be given a briefing to explain where the track goes and what the different marshalls flags mean. Start each session slowly and give your tyres time to warm up. Most accidents happen on cold tyres, where the rider gets a bit giddy at the start of a session. Use the day's early sessions to learn where the track goes and the best lines through the turns.

Groups usually go out for 15 to 20 minutes at a time. Doesn't sound like long, but it's long enough when you're concentrating and exerting plenty of physical energy. The hardest part is waiting until it's the turn of your group to go out again. Trackdays can be draining, so keep fluid levels up by drinking plenty of water and eat little and often – high-energy foods such as snack bars are ideal.

If you want to accelerate the learning curve, think about going to a race school. Structures vary, but most assign an instructor (usually a professional racer) to groups of roughly the same ability (typically no more than five riders, and sometimes one-to-one). A race school is the best way to work towards quick results on specific aspects of your riding, and you may not even need to use your own bike since some schools provide the machines.

Approached properly, trackdays and race schools will improve your machine control, which can only add to your riding skills and enjoyment. Check the bike press and the internet or ask your local bike dealer for details of events. And be warned: trackdays are addictive...

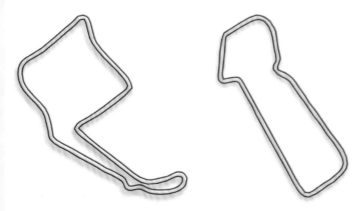

Oulton Park

Snetterton

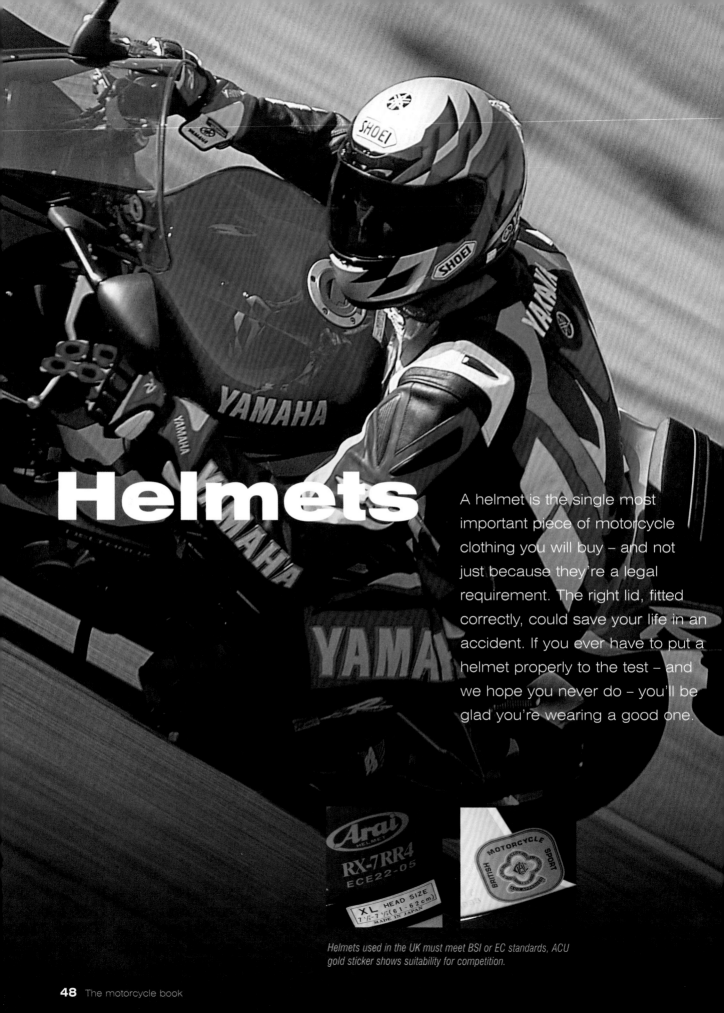

Helmets

A helmet is the single most important piece of motorcycle clothing you will buy – and not just because they're a legal requirement. The right lid, fitted correctly, could save your life in an accident. If you ever have to put a helmet properly to the test – and we hope you never do – you'll be glad you're wearing a good one.

Helmets used in the UK must meet BSI or EC standards, ACU gold sticker shows suitability for competition.

There's no need to spend a fortune to get a helmet that will provide an adequate level of protection. All helmets sold in the UK have to comply to a baseline standard to be legal for road use. More expensive helmets meet exactly the same standards as cheaper ones, the differences being in more complex construction, increased comfort and the quality and complexity of finish, visor mechanism, vents, liner material, removable liners and so on.

After the strap that holds your helmet on (usually a seatbelt-type or a pair of D-rings through which the strap passes), the next most important components are the outer shell and inner liner. Outer shells are usually injection-moulded polycarbonate (normally, but not always, used at the lower end of the market) or a laminate of glass fibre, carbon fibre and Kevlar. The outer shell is there to resist abrasion and penetration of objects in an impact.

The inner is moulded polystyrene designed to deform on impact, absorbing the force of a blow. For this reason, helmets that have sustained an impact should be replaced, or at least inspected – they're designed to take only one hefty hit. Inside the inner is a foam-backed cloth liner. This has no protective value but is there for comfort only. The helmet must fit your head evenly without excessive pressure at any point. If there is pressure, try another size or make.

Many helmets have vents to allow cool air in and warm air out, which is intended to reduce visor misting. There are anti-mist preparations and laminates available to help minimise this almost inevitable problem of full-face helmets. Laminates provide longer-term protection than sprays which have to be regularly applied.

Never let your helmet roll around on the floor; stand it with the head aperture to the ground. Use only very mild detergents and polish on lids, since solvents can attack shells and visors. Never buy a second-hand helmet – you don't know its history and it could have been dropped. Some helmets are quieter than others, but none are so quiet as to prevent hearing damage from wind noise – so always wear ear plugs.

The current British Standard for helmets (BS6658) is being phased out in favour of the European ECE22-05. The BS sticker will continue to appear on the back of lids for the next few years. The EC standard is denoted on a label on the chin strap, although some manufacturers are also declaring it on the outside of the shell. Gold ACU stickers show that a helmet has been approved for competition use (the tag is silver for off-road lids).

Reckon to replace your helmet every four to five years, regardless of how well you've looked after it, because the materials that make up your lid degrade over time. And always replace scratched visors as soon as possible.

Full-face helmets provide the most protection.

Motocross lids make for urban cool on the road.

Scooter, retro and classic riders often favour open-face.

Many excellent, high-tech man-made materials are now being used in motorcycle clothing. But when it comes to crash protection, particularly from abrasion, there's still nothing to top good old-fashioned leather – especially when those leathers have state-of-the-art armour built in. Back in 1995, EC legislation called the Personal Protective Equipment (PPE) Directive was introduced, and this is your guarantee that your leathers will do what you hope they'll do. Leathers cannot be sold as protective clothing – as opposed to merely fashion items – in Britain and the rest of Europe, unless their design and construction have passed a British or European Standard or similar approved test. They must also have passed an EC examination. Manufacturers must have EC-approved quality control processes in place too. Only then can leathers carry a CE tag to show they're up to scratch.

Leathers

Two-piece on the left from Aprilia's range. Plenty of integral armour and the pieces zip together. One-piece suit on right looks the racing part with velcro for knee sliders.

All the colours, all the shapes, this Spyke suit's top level kit.

While leather is very good for sliding along in, it doesn't have much in-built impact protection. That's why it pays to have decent armour at likely impact points – shoulders, elbows, back, hips and knees. Some cheap leathers (and indeed some more expensive ones) have foam padding in these areas. That isn't going to help much in a crash. Proper armour, designed to absorb some of the energy of an impact, will.

Armour is usually made of two or more materials – a harder outer layer made of dense foam or plastic, and a softer inner. The outer layer spreads the load across the inner, which cushions the impact. Decent armour finds the middle ground between too hard – which only serves to deflect the shock of impact directly to your body, and too soft, which will do the same.

As with the leathers that carry the armour, there are EC standards for armour sold as protective equipment, so the CE tag offers some guarantee of the protective potential. For more detail on armour, see page 62.

With the object of getting decent leathers in mind, there's only one choice left – one-piece or two-piece? A one-piece gives instant racer chic, but unlike a two-piece you can't just slip the jacket off when you reach your destination. Two-piece

suits usually zip together, and the further round your waist that zip extends, the better it will hold together in the event of a tumble.

One-piece suits are widely viewed as offering superior protection. That is not always the case – there are good and bad suits in each category. Look for good quality hide, double layers (panels should be sewn on rather than sewn in) and armour on impact points.

If your leathers get wet, let them dry out naturally, otherwise the material and stitching can weaken. Should they become dirty, clean them with a very mild detergent solution and, again, allow them to dry naturally. There are many leather treatments on the market, but some of them are better suited to horse saddles than bike suits. Use sparingly and don't soak stitching with them, at the risk of weakening it. And don't be tempted to use waterproofing solutions on leather for the same reasons. Carry waterproofs (page 58) to wear on top when the clouds open, which given our uncertain weather, they almost certainly will.

Good leathers cost but, just like a decent helmet, they're more than worth it. Looked after properly they will last and, more importantly, protect you for years. Only the colours and styling go out of date.

Another two-piece. This time there are zips right round the waist.

Man-made fabric
jackets & trousers

A fabric jacket can be as stylish as leathers.

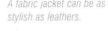

Waist belt keeps wind from upper body. Good neck closure too.

Plenty of armour and upper-arm straps. Good.

Here's the basic set-up. Look for decent armour, an effective neck closure, and straps at key points to make the suit fit you. Outer pockets need double closures to keep rain out, and your possessions in.

Lots of armour again. And a pocket for the mobile phone.

Leather might provide the ultimate in crash protection, but other than wind protection, it struggles to keep out the other elements. That's where fabric jackets and trousers come into their own. What's more, modern materials and armour mean they can run leathers a close second when things go pear-shaped.

There's a huge array of fabric clothing available, at all prices. What the clothing costs isn't always an indication of how water/wind/crash-proof it'll be, but features such as armour, thermal and waterproof linings made of space-age materials and features like pockets and vents all tend to drive prices up.

Fit is all important. Jacket sleeves must be long enough so they don't ride up with arms outstretched; likewise the back and trouser legs when you're crouched in riding position. If you expect to wear the jacket over winter layers or one-piece leathers, it has to be roomy, but ideally not so baggy as to flap around with the thermal liner removed on warmer days. Trousers and jackets that zip together are preferable to those which don't, not only for warmth, but also to prevent them parting company and exposing your flesh in a crash. Adjustable straps on the collar, waist, wrists, elbows and ankles help ensure the best fit. Flaps over zips help keep wind and water out, and check that the poppers nearest the waist and crotch are rubber-covered to prevent damage to tank paintwork.

Armour, preferably CE-approved, is fitted in many fabric jackets and trousers, and is usually removable to allow the garments to be worn over leathers containing armour of their own. When you try on a jacket or trousers, make sure that the armour isn't too free to move around. It needs to stay close to the areas it is designed to protect or else it won't be much use in a crash.

As with leathers, double stitching and layers are definite bonuses on impact points like elbows and posterior. Fabrics lack the durability of leather, so it's pretty much a foregone conclusion that you'll knock holes in them even in low-speed spills.

Most modern jackets and trousers have a waterproof membrane under the outer – look for Gore-Tex and Sympatex labels. These fabrics keep moisture out while allowing sweat to escape.

So while decent fabric clothing should keep you warm and dry, it won't provide ultimate crash protection. But it's certainly better than simple nylon waterproofs, which are very much a second line of defence on top of proper protective clothing.

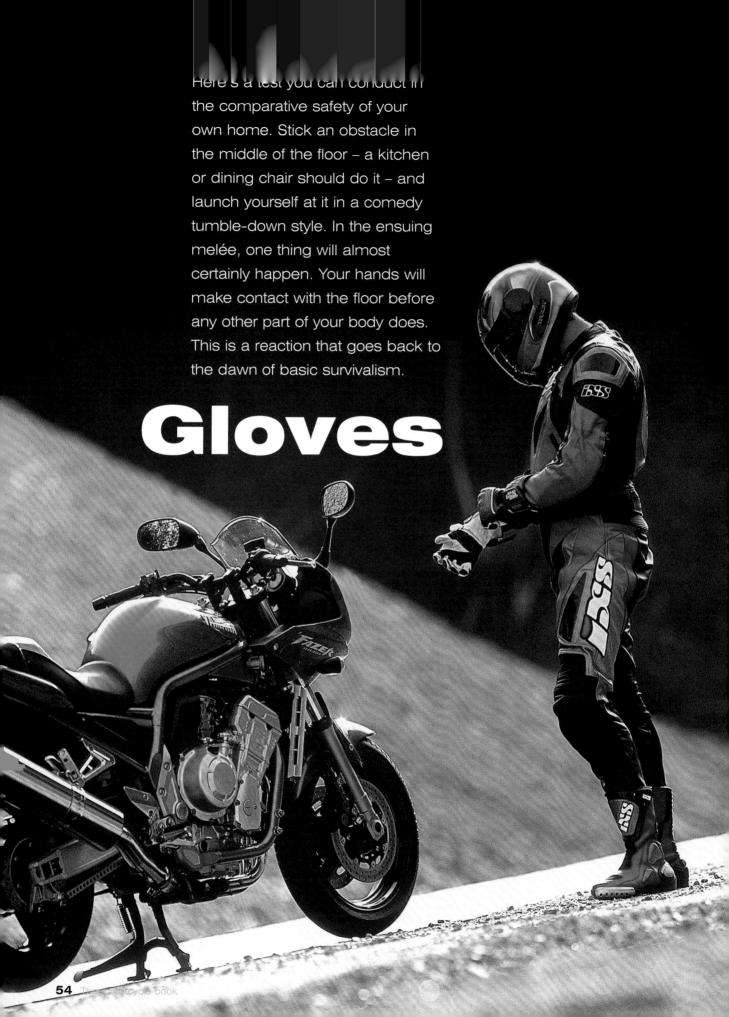

Here's a test you can conduct in the comparative safety of your own home. Stick an obstacle in the middle of the floor – a kitchen or dining chair should do it – and launch yourself at it in a comedy tumble-down style. In the ensuing melée, one thing will almost certainly happen. Your hands will make contact with the floor before any other part of your body does. This is a reaction that goes back to the dawn of basic survivalism.

Gloves

Consider that your hands shoot out first in a fall, and be assured that gloveless, T-shirted, shorts-wearing, trainer-shoed casual summer riders are cruising for much more than a bruising. It isn't called protective clothing for nothing, and after a decent helmet, proper gloves are the next most essential line of defence.

At their most basic, gloves must let you still feel the controls through their protective layers. Leather is great for this. It breaks in nicely and moulds to the shape of your hands and their movement. Double layer leather and stitched-in protection should be there at impact points – specifically, palms and knuckles. As with most bike clothing, hi-tech materials are being used more extensively, such as Kevlar, Cordura and Thinsulate for, variously, protection, weatherproofing and insulation. Many modern gloves are a combination of leather and these hi-tech fabrics. Some are made wholly from non-leather materials.

Look for velcro wrist straps and do them up tight enough for the gloves to stay on your hands in the event of a tumble.

When buying gloves, it's a good idea to take along your leathers or jacket to check for fit over or under the cuffs.

As the seasons change, so will your glove requirements. In their better made (and usually more expensive) forms, race and summer gloves offer optimal feel of controls and great crash protection but poor insulation from rain and cold weather. Waterproof and windproof but breathable gloves are now available for all-weather riding, and insulated gloves keep out the chill on the coldest days.

If your leather gloves do get wet, let them dry naturally rather than putting them on top of a radiator or in the airing cupboard.

Basic race-style glove, note knuckle protection and long wrist.

Shorty race glove. Good hand protection, elasticated wrist.

Lots of carbon and kevlar in these Spidis. Fine leather for good feel, but no wrist staps.

Double layers, over-and-under the wrist staps, loads of protective inserts. Plenty of protection for even the most paranoid.

Boots

Decent bike boots are an important part of your protective clothing wardrobe. As well as your foot, they should also protect the ankle and lower leg, which are particularly vulnerable.

Leather is still the most common material used in bike boots but, as with clothing, many hi-tech fabrics are being used – and not just for the linings.

Race-style boots usually have impact protection in the shin, ankle, calf and heel areas. Foam is the minimum to look for and additional armour, made from high-impact plastic for example, is a definite bonus. To prevent them flexing in a tumble, soles are often reinforced with metal or plastic inserts, which still allow the sole to give when the wearer is walking. Zip closures are normally concealed behind a Velcro flap to reduce the chances of their opening in an impact and the boot flying off.

Full-on race boots come with toe and calf sliders and most flex sufficiently to make walking around in them reasonably easy. However, there's a rule of thumb that says the more protective a boot, the less comfortable it is off the bike. Not always true, but you certainly wouldn't want to go on a nature ramble in motocross boots.

Touring-style boots offer more of a compromise. Many give good levels of protection with the added bonus of a degree of waterproofing, although some sports boots are now also available with this. Touring boots are usually pretty comfortable off the bike.

Winter boots go even further, offering insulation too. As with gloves, this is important for winter riding. Most of your body's heat is lost through the extremities. Apart from being uncomfortable, coldness can result in reduced concentration or worse, especially when the wind-chill factor is taken into consideration.

Most riders wind up with several pairs of boots to suit the seasons or the type of riding they're doing.

When choosing boots, take your riding suit or trousers with you to ensure they zip up okay over your leathers or under your oversuit. Like gloves, boots should always be allowed to dry naturally to preserve the leather.

Above and below, the simple, clean lines of touring boots can conceal a multitude of weatherproof fabrics.

Motocross boots; very protective, but very stiff for everyday use.

Race boots provide optimum support for least weight.

Back in the bad old days, waterproof clothing meant waxed cotton. And it did a reasonable enough job for the speeds of the day, but it also required continual reproofing and was an absolute dirt magnet. It's still available, but unless you're on some kind of retro trip, you may like to consider something a bit more up-to-date.

Waterproofs

Then there were PVC oversuits. Waterproof all right (until they ripped along their welded seams), but the build-up of sweat on the inside, even on mild days, could make you as sodden as the rain you were trying to keep out.

Nylon is a popular material for waterproofs and has the advantage of folding down small so they can be carried easily, often in an integral bum bag.

Nowadays, though, modern synthetics allow oversuits to pull off that neat trick of being waterproof and breathable at the same time. A real bonus on warm days or when riding any distance. Many suits are lined for additional protection from the cold. Some feature reflective material to boost your visibility at night.

Check that seams are taped on the inside to stop water seeping through. Zips should also have Velcro flaps to prevent water getting in through the closures. And these closures should open sufficiently wide to allow you to get into the suit at the side of the road once the heavens have opened. Choose a suit large enough to go over your usual riding gear, and make sure it's big enough not to restrict your riding position when it's on, but not so big as to flap around like a gigantic sail on the move. Velcro ankle, wrist and neck closures help to fit the suit snugly to your body and prevent water entering through these key areas.

Waterproof overboots and gloves are also available and are worth it if you think you're going to get caught out by the weather while wearing your summer gear. They fold down so small that they take up next to no space under your bike's seat.

Waterproof suits can carry armour too and boast many features of their less rain-stopping equivalents. As with any bike clothing, look for good fit.

Handy nylon one-piece can be carried in integral bum-bag 'til needed.

Thermals

Cold can be one of the rider's biggest enemies. Once you get chilly, your concentration starts to wander and accidents can happen. Even when the weather's just above zero degrees, wind chill can take the temperature you're enduring well down into the negative numbers. Apart from all that, it's just downright miserable, and biking's meant to be fun. But with the right gear, year-round riding needn't be a freezing chore.

Just make sure you take this beauty off before going into the bank.

Thermal fleece is something you'll be grateful for.

Thermal trousers – forget style, it's keeping warm that counts. Thermals make a huge difference in cold weather.

Face and neck protector.

Tabard to cover neck and chest.

Fingers get cold first without thermal gloves.

Balaclava extends to upper body.

You could raid grandad's underwear drawer for a pair of long johns and long-sleeved vest, because they'll serve you pretty well. Thermal underwear is available in most high street clothing chain stores at reasonable prices. More specialised thermals can be had from skiing and outdoor shops too.

Natural materials work well until they get wet, either from sweat or rain, when they tend to hold on to the moisture and take an age to dry out. That's when cold can set in again. Silk is lighter and thinner than cotton or wool, so it tends to work better in this respect. Full synthetics tend to let body heat build up and up, which can be pretty uncomfortable too. One other problem is that synthetics often cause worse abrasions than natural fabrics in the event of a tumble.

Bike clothing manufacturers are wise to the problems and offer a variety of solutions, some of which combine natural and synthetic materials. These allow you to keep warm or cool as required, wicking sweat away from the body in the process.

A thermal neck warmer is a real boon on colder days, filling the vulnerable gap between jacket collar and helmet. A thin thermal balaclava under your helmet is a great help too. As for the other extremities most prone to heat loss, thermal socks and inner gloves are indispensable.

Thermal clothing might just seem like another layer of protection to struggle in and out of, but on long cold rides, you'll be glad you bothered.

Armour

Leathers and man-made fabric suits provide varying degrees of abrasion protection, but neither offers the rider much impact protection. That's where armour comes into play. It can make the difference between serious injury and walking away from a tumble.

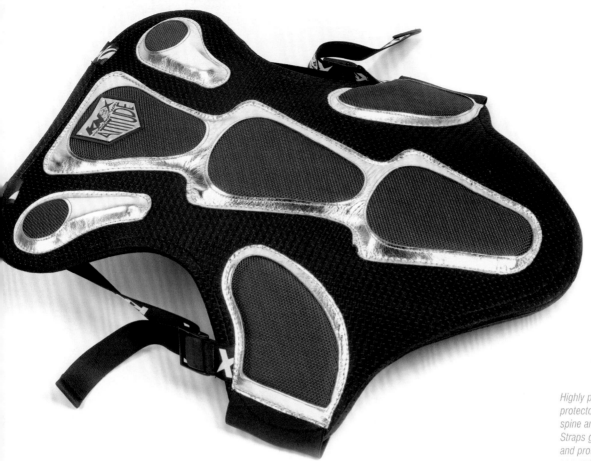

Highly protective Knox back protector covering shoulder, spine and kidney areas. Straps go over shoulders and protector is further secured by velcro waist belt.

Simple foam padding provides little if any protection. The most it does is to make suits more comfortable. Armour proper varies in hardness. Too unforgiving, and it transfers the shock of impact directly to the body. Too soft and the same thing happens. Good armour lies between these extremes and often has harder (outer) and softer (inner) elements, because it needs to take the initial impact, then deform to soften the blow as much as it can. It's very similar to what happens with a crash helmet (see page 48), where the hard outer takes the initial whack and prevents penetration of objects, and the soft, deformable inner cushions the impact. In theory, then, the inside of the lid quickly slows the rider's head to a stop, rather than the sudden contact with the ground.

Armour sold as protective equipment must comply to CE tests and carry a label accordingly, just as with leathers. Look for the label and then at least you'll know your money is being invested in something that meets certain base standards. Good armour is designed to pass as little as 30 per cent of the force of an impact. As with helmets, replace any armour that's taken a significant whack in a crash. That's fairly simple on most riding suits, since it's held in Velcro-fastened pockets in the lining.

Check that armour is in the right place on any suit you're thinking of buying – not just where it's located (knees, hips, elbows, shoulders and back), but also how it fits to your body.

Many riders use a separate back protector to give extra peace of mind. For comfort, you'll need to remove the one in your suit, if it has one. First developed for the race track, back protectors have saved many riders from severe injury.

State-of-the-art armour inserts

Above and right, motocross armour

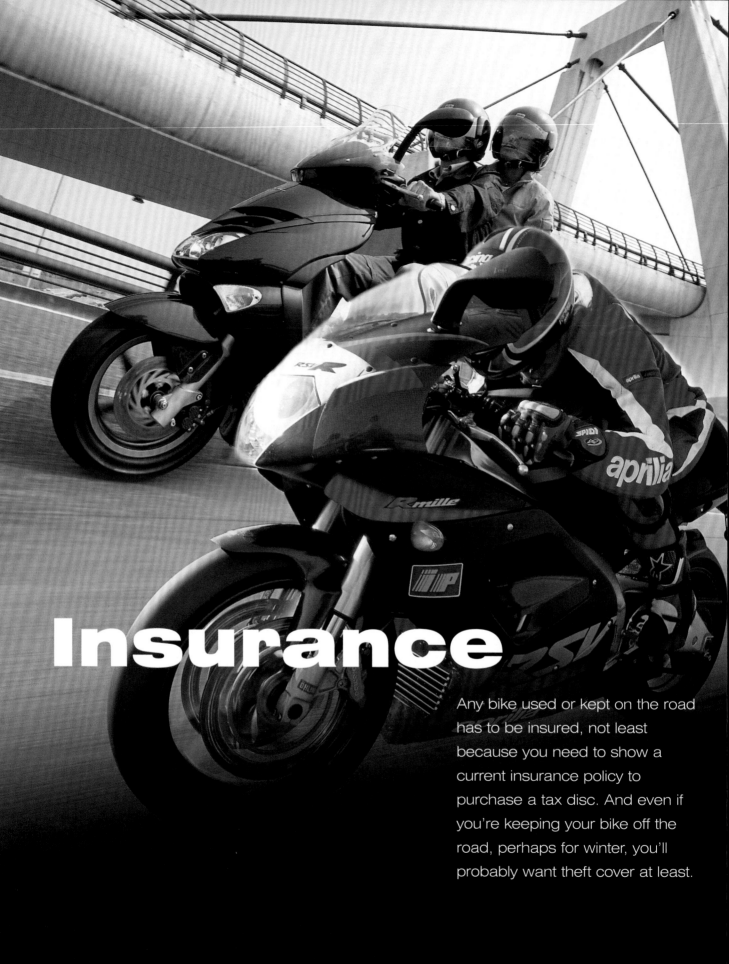

Insurance

Any bike used or kept on the road has to be insured, not least because you need to show a current insurance policy to purchase a tax disc. And even if you're keeping your bike off the road, perhaps for winter, you'll probably want theft cover at least.

There are three main types of insurance cover: third party only; third party, fire and theft; and comprehensive. Cost rises in line with level of cover.

Third party only is the basic legal minimum required to get you on the road. In the event of your causing an accident, it covers injury to other people and damage to their vehicles. It doesn't cover injury or damage to you or your bike and, obviously, fire and theft are excluded.

Third party, fire and theft provides broader cover. Apart from third party liabilities being taken care of, if your bike is destroyed by fire (not that they often combust, spontaneously or otherwise) your insurers will pay out. More importantly, you're covered against theft of your bike, provided you meet the security conditions set out in your policy. But you are not covered for any damage caused to the bike and/or your helmet and leathers through an accident where you're at fault. For that, you'll need comprehensive insurance, but even this doesn't go so far as to cover personal injury claims or loss of earnings where the accident is down to you.

Insurance companies look at a variety of factors in calculating your premium, or even to decide if they want to cover you at all. Your age, how long you've held a full licence, occupation, address, any motoring convictions, previous claims, where the bike will be kept and, of course, the type of bike – all these factors have a bearing on how much your insurance cover will cost.

The cost of insurance tends to drop at the ages of 21, 25 and 35. A 19-year-old pop musician with a Suzuki GSX-R1000, no garage, a dangerous driving conviction, who has held a full licence for only one year and lives in an inner city, is unlikely to find an insurer willing to cover them. Even if an insurer will, the premium is likely to be prohibitively expensive. At the other extreme, a 55-year-old parish priest in a rural outpost, with a commuter bike, a garage and a clean licence for 35 years, is likely to have an easier time of it.

Most riders fall between these extremes of course, and there is much you can do to reduce your premium so it pays to shop around. Insurance policies, apart from third party only, have an 'excess', an initial amount of any claim you agree to pay yourself. If you agree to pay a higher excess, your insurer will reduce the premium. Similarly, you can reduce your premium by garaging your bike, fitting an approved alarm or immobiliser, and using additional locks and data tagging. It's worth taking all the anti-theft precautions that you can. Insurers often refuse theft cover to people who've had machines stolen when they eventually get their replacement bikes.

No-claims discount can make a huge difference to your premium – up to 50 per cent if you can maintain a clean insurance record for five years.

Above all, remember to play it straight with your insurer. If you make any major modifications to your bike, you must tell them or they could refuse to pay out on a claim. And they do keep a register of claims and investigate any dubious claims vigorously.

Most important of all, make sure you can get insurance cover for the bike you want *before* committing to buying it. If you can't, all's not lost. Go for a bike in a lower insurance group that you can get cover for (bikes are graded according to type, performance and how attractive they are to thieves) and do your best to build a good insurance record.

Both ends of the risk scale as perceived by the insurance companies. Of course the truth lies somewhere between...

Bad: *young, inner city, big bike, expensive to insure.*

Good: *old, small bike, more no-claims than nostril hairs!*

Security

Bike theft statistics make pretty depressing reading. In the UK alone, 30,000 bikes are stolen every year – that's one every 20 minutes or so. Precious few are ever recovered. Physical security of machines is not high on bike manufacturers' list of priorities. The best you can expect as standard on most bikes is a steering lock on the ignition barrel incapable of withstanding anything more than a half-hearted attempt with a screwdriver. A sharp tug on the bars is enough to pop some. So that's the bad news. But take heart – there's still plenty you can do to reduce the chances of becoming part of the statistics.

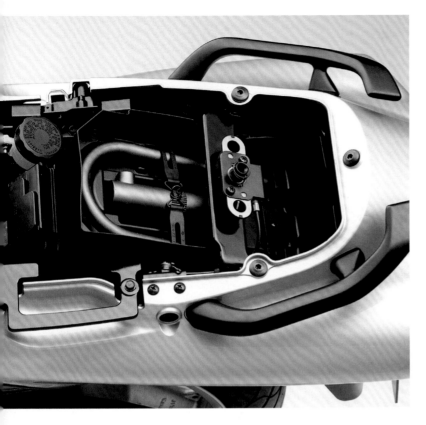

U-locks and cables can often be stored under the seat.

If you're able to park your bike where you can see it while you go about your business, so much the better. This is rarely practical, though, so you'll need additional protection.

Always use a lock of some sort, no matter how short a time you're leaving your bike unattended. A disc lock is easy to carry and provides some amount of visible deterrent, hopefully enough to put off casual joyriders while you nip into the shop for a newspaper. But it won't stop more determined thieves lifting your bike into a van.

A U-lock is bulkier and less easy to carry, but provides a similar level of security by passing through the brake discs at the fork legs to prevent the bike being wheeled away. Some are large enough, or come with a cable, to secure the bike to another machine or an immovable object, such as a lamp post. Many modern bikes have a space under the seat for a U-lock, or there are carrying brackets that mount behind the numberplate or on the frame.

The next step up is a high-quality lock and chain that will allow you secure the bike to an immovable object. But while they provide a higher level of security, the larger they are, the more difficult they are to carry. They can be strapped in a bag on the pillion seat or carried in a tank bag or panniers, but for safety's sake don't be tempted to carry a lock and chain around your waist or over your shoulder.

When locking up, take care not to thread the chain through a part of the bike that can be easily removed, such as a footrest hanger, otherwise you might come back to the bike to find yourself with no

more than a solidly secured brake pedal. And if locking one of the wheels to the immovable object, be sure to wrap the chain round the rim rather than one of the spokes. Don't leave so much slack in the chain that its links (or the lock itself) can reach the ground, where they'll be all the easier for a thief to attack with a hammer.

While an alarm should be enough to put off a casual thief, it can't stop your bike being lifted into a van. Neither can an immobiliser, but it can stop it being ridden away. Many insurance companies insist you fit one of these electronic security devices as a condition of your insurance cover. Even where their fitment is not a pre-condition, insurers usually offer a discount if you fit one that's on their approved list of alarms and immobilisers. And as they usually self-arm when you park the bike up, they're one part of your security routine you won't forget. Sadly, though, most people ignore the screeches and bleeps of vehicle alarms these days, so you'll need to employ some form of physical security too.

Where you park is as important as what you do once you've parked. Busy, well-lit areas are best – even the most brazen thieves prefer a little privacy.

Be aware that thieves often follow their targets to see where they're going to park or where they live. Don't get paranoid. But if you suspect you're being tailed, there's no harm in going round the block one more time just to be sure.

When you're parking at work, try to arrange for you and a colleague to lock your bikes together. If

Getting heavy duty with big gauge chain and lock.

enough of you ride to work, your employers might agree to let you use part of a warehouse to park in, or fit ground anchors in the car park for your bikes. And make the security guys aware of your bike, then at least they'll know if the person taking an interest in the machine isn't you.

Some local authorities have fitted anchors in bike bays. Use them whenever possible.

If your only option is to park outside, you might want to consider using a bike cover, which at least hides the bike from casual prying eyes. The more weathered and knackered the cover looks, the better. There could be any old junk under there.

All the advice on parking when you're out also applies at home, if you don't have the luxury of a shed or garage. If you have a back garden, park your bike there in preference to out front.

The safest place to store your bike is a secure shed or garage, and it may be a condition of your insurance that it's locked up at night. It's best to put your bike away as soon as you get home, and don't spend ages warming it up outside your house before you go out. Maintenance and cleaning are best done out of view too, or done quickly. And don't advertise the fact that you're a bike fan by plastering your garage or shed doors with bike stickers.

Fit a ground anchor in your shed or garage. Position it so it's difficult for a thief to access when

the bike's parked up and thread the chain through the frame or swingarm and back wheel rather than through the front. Again, make sure the chain is taut enough to be clear of the floor and the lock is positioned so that it can't be pulled to the ground and smacked with a hammer.

Make your garage or shed doors secure too. The popular up-and-over metal garage doors are as easy to pop open as a can of beer. Fit extra deadlocks, but not to the extent of advertising the fact that there's something worth nicking in there. Additional locks are best fitted on the inside of the door, where possible.

If your garage is adjacent to the house, and you have a domestic alarm system, consider extending it to the garage. Should your garage or shed have electricity on the same ring as the house, you could use a cheap baby monitor for extra peace of mind.

No one likes talking about bike theft, but security is as essential to the motorcyclist as decent riding kit. Just ask anyone who's been unfortunate enough to lose a bike to theft.

Remember, the biggest threat of theft comes not from the casual thief or joyrider, but the professional thief, many of whom steal to order. Do what you can to put both classes of scum out of business.

As almost three-quarters of stolen bikes are broken up to be sold on as spares, there's one

more security precaution that might put potential thieves off – marking systems such as Datatag. Tagging makes the rightful owner of stolen parts easier to trace. It uses marking numbers, microdots or microchip tags stamped on or fitted to various of the bike's components. These codes are unique to each owner, which allows the owner's name and address to be traced through a database when the stolen parts are found by the police. Police forces are equipped with scanners to read microchip tags, and tagging can provide the law with the evidence to convict bike thieves.

This is one area of security where many manufacturers are beginning to do more for the purchasers of their bikes, even if these companies are still woefully lax on physical security. Many new bikes come with Datatag or similar as standard. Honda is using a marking system called Smart Water. The company has also introduced a concept called HISS (Honda Ignition Security System), a type of immobiliser that will only allow the bike to be started with the correct key.

If your bike doesn't have tagging, buy a kit from your dealer and mark key components yourself, placing the sticker that comes with the kit on the screen or top of the tank to advertise that you've done it. If you've bought a Datatagged bike second-hand, the previous owner should be able to give you the documentation to register yourself with the company as the new owner.

Don't become a paranoid obsessive about bike security, but be wary. Take as many steps as you reasonably can to protect your bike. Above all, use the best quality gear (look for the Sold Secure and *RiDE* magazine recommended tags on new products, or ask the advice of your local police vehicle security unit and/or insurance company). With a little care and common sense, you can put bike theft lower down your list of worries.

One last thing: we can all do our bit to stop theft by not buying bikes or parts we suspect to be stolen. Take away the demand and the supply will dwindle.

Keep your garage secure, but do it with discreet, internal locks like these (above) so as not to advertise what you've got.

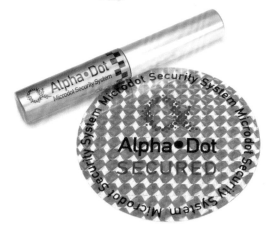

Security is getting smarter, but so are thieves.

Fit an alarm/imobiliser as a first-line deterrent.

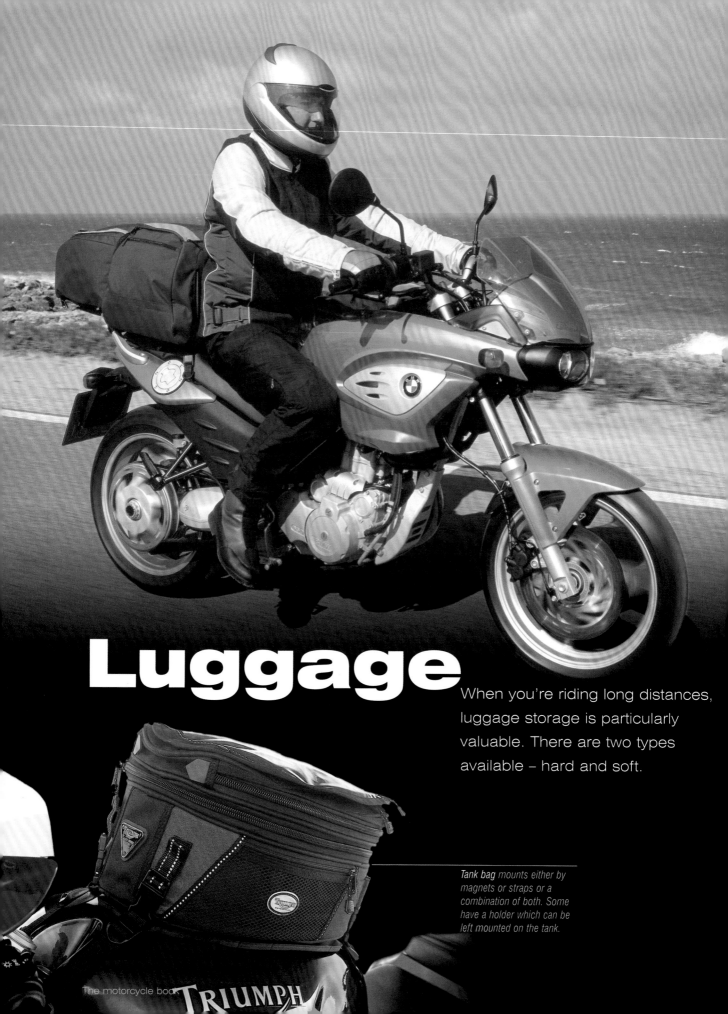

Luggage

When you're riding long distances, luggage storage is particularly valuable. There are two types available – hard and soft.

Tank bag mounts either by magnets or straps or a combination of both. Some have a holder which can be left mounted on the tank.

Ventura Bike Pac *can be used as a rucksack off the bike. This is better than a conventional rucksack as you don't have to carry weight on your back while riding.*

B-Bag *mounts over the pillion seat. Design means some weight can be carried lower down.*

Frank Thomas Cargo *hard luggage is favoured by some for its robustness. Less easy to store off the bike, however.*

Hard luggage is available as an option from some bike manufacturers and there is a healthy aftermarket making hard-shelled panniers and top boxes. Some is available colour-matched to your bike's paint scheme. The units are mounted on frames bolted to the bike and can be removed when you arrive at your destination. Most are lockable for limited security when you stop en route.

Soft luggage offers a degree more flexibility than hard luggage, in that it can be easily moved from bike to bike and doesn't need bolted on framework, which can look unsightly when hard boxes are removed.

There are various types of soft luggage. Tank bags have magnetic bases to attach them to the fuel tank, with straps for additional security or for using on plastic tanks. Some are expandable by means of a concertina system of fabric and zips. Others have straps and double up as rucksacks. Clear panels on top allow you to refer to maps or directions.

Throwover panniers attach over the seat by a system of straps and laces. Some are shaped to accomodate the kicked-up silencers of sportsbikes. There are tail packs too, which bungy on to the pillion pad. Others mount on racks at the back of the bike. Panniers and tail packs are often expandable. The better soft luggage comes with rain covers that look like gigantic shower caps.

There are two main things to remember with luggage. The first is to ensure that it's securely mounted and doesn't hamper operation of the bike. Your trip will come to an unscheduled and unpleasant stop if soft panniers, for example, find their way into the back wheel. It's also surprising how much heat silencers generate, enough to set panniers and their contents smouldering nicely.

The second thing to remember is that you shouldn't overload luggage. Too much weight wrongly distributed will upset the handling of your bike. Your owner's manual will tell you how much can be safely carried. At a more basic level, cram too much into the bags and there's a chance they'll burst open. But if you don't mind airing your dirty linen on the M25, then that's up to you.

Throw-over soft panniers
These are from Triumph. Straps and bungees hold them on. Note how they're shaped so as not to touch the kicked-up silencers.

Useful
Gadgets

We're not talking here about simple customising. Instead, we're interested in more handy accessories than Live-to-Ride bolt-ons, tinted headlamp covers, anodised bolts and myriad other tat that gets in between the useful pages of so many accessory catalogues. The engine and chassis sections of this book look at the key items you might consider in those departments, so over the next couple of pages we'll turn our attentions to those items which will improve your biking life in more general and useful ways.

Paddock stands/benches
Few bikes come with centre stands these days. They're options on some and almost a religious no-no on others, particularly sportsbikes. Centre stands make work on a bike easy where wheel removal is required (albeit with the assistance of bottle jacks and arbitrary bits of wood for the front), but in their absence, paddock stands make sense.
Rear paddock stands raise

the back wheel off the floor by holding the swing arm or rear wheel spindle, while front stands raise the forks to bring the front wheel clear. Others, meanwhile, sit under the bottom yoke to hold the bike up in the absence of the front end.
Other stands are available to go under the engine and lift the whole bike up. Going the whole distance, you can buy a hydraulic bench to lift your bike close to eye level for intensive maintenance.

Intercoms *'Hello, hello, are you there? Go ahead London. Did you see that guy? Are we there yet? Slow down. Speed up. Scream if you want to go faster.' Yes, intercoms are endless fun and make riding more sociable. And when the novelty pales, you can always unplug them.*

Tank protectors
These handy little items don't cost much, but spare your tank's finish from the worst your jacket or leathers have to inflict. Depending on the tolerance of your taste, you can choose clear or self-coloured to something with silicone breasts on. But they all work the same.

Battery chargers
If your bike's going to be laid up for any length of time, and there's power in your shed, buy a trickle charger to keep your battery up to power. Otherwise it'll be dead and useless come springtime.

Fasteners
By all means use aftermarket ally fasteners where they don't compromise structural integrity or come under extreme pressure – for example, holding on brake calipers. They save weight, look trick and corrode more slowly than some badly plated original equipment stuff.

Aftermarket bodywork, mirrors, indicators, levers
The first parts to take the flak in a tumble are also highly expensive. If you aren't a stickler for originality, a healthy aftermarket provides more affordable options. Bodywork, mirrors, indicators and levers are all available in varying quality, but almost always at lower prices than original parts from a dealer. Track bike addicts have no qualms about fitting this kit, because it mostly works. Hugger (above) is a useful bolt-on that stops road dirt and water being flung at the rear shock by the back wheel.

Tyre pressure gauges
As anyone who's struggled with garage forecourt air lines and gauges will attest (see Tyres), they were designed by an anti-biking devil who laughs diabolically as your 20p or token runs out. A foot pump and a decent analogue or digital gauge are much better bets to keep pressures spot-on.

Know your motorcycle

Tyres

You aren't going anywhere without tyres, and they're arguably the most important parts of a motorcycle, with some of the toughest jobs to do. The rear transmits the power to the ground, while both have a huge part to play in the handling of the bike, offering grip in the turns as well as in a straight line. This grip is also vital for efficient braking.

Fit the correct tyres for your bike and type of the riding you do – and don't be tempted to mix and match brands or types.

Tyres do plenty for us and ask for little in return. Don't take them for granted. Check every week that they're at your bike manufacturer's recommended pressures. Do this when they're cold. Your machine manual will tell you the correct pressures for solo, pillion and riding with luggage.

Under-inflation accelerates wear, ruins handling, raises fuel consumption and lowers top speed. Over-inflation makes the ride less comfortable and reduces the size of the patch of tyre in contact with the road, upsetting handling. It can also lead to premature wear. So it pays to get tyre pressures right, although anyone who's ever struggled to inflate their bike tyres with a garage forecourt air line will understand why people neglect them. Best to get a footpump and a decent tyre pressure gauge – and don't trust the cheap plastic item on top of most footpumps.

Remember to replace the valve caps. At higher speeds, centrifugal forces can have the same effect on a valve stem as putting your finger on it. The only thing stopping the air escaping is the valve cap. Metal ones with rubber seals inside are best for motorcycle applications.

Wear indicators – little raised ridges across and in the bottom of the tread grooves – show when your tyres have reached the end of the manufacturer's recommended safe wear limit. Little arrows or the letters TWI (tread wear indicator) at the 'shoulder' or top of the tyre wall indicate the grooves they're in.

Occasionally, other damage such as punctures or tears might mean they need to be changed before they wear out. It's a good idea before every ride to check for punctures and tears, or any foreign objects such as glass or nails stuck in the tread. There is another thing that might lead to early replacement, especially if your regular riding doesn't feature many corners. That's when the tyres 'square off' – the tyres lose their semi-circular profile at the centre of the tread.

Fit the correct type of tyres to your bike, look after them and they'll look after you.

Tyre types

There are three main tyre types – crossply, bias-belted and radial. These days crossplies are mainly found on lighter, slower bikes, although they are available with up to a 130mph-plus rating for some bikes. Bias-belts were developed for the emerging class of superbikes in the 1970s and are still fairly popular. But radials are the most modern construction.

As well as being the most modern, radial construction is fast becoming the most popular tyre type – you'll find nothing else on sportsbikes. Radials almost always run without inner tubes.

In a crossply, the plies that make up the carcass cross the circumference at around 25–35° and are layered to criss-cross each other. A bias-belted tyre has additional plies under the crown (the treaded rubber bit) to prevent centrifugal expansion under load and slow wear.

The plies in a radial tyre run at 90° across the circumference, with what are called crown plies running at more oblique angles to maintain the profile, a bit like the older bias belts do.

Apart from the carcass, there are elements common to all tyres. The bead or tringle is made from wire and holds the tyre to the rim. The bead filler is a rubber insert that helps strengthen the sidewall – the area between the bead and the crown, which is the treaded rubber section. The shoulder is where the sidewall meets the crown.

Tyres come in different compounds of rubber that are invariably a compromise between grip and longevity. Tourer riders will want longevity over ultra-grippiness, while the sportsbike rider seeking to make the most of the bike's handling will want grip above anything else. Some tyres even have multiple compounds on the crown – hard and long-wearing in the middle, softer on the edges for the turns.

Although it's important, compound is not the single most vital aspect of a tyre. It's the carcass that's the busiest part of the tyre. A mix of various synthetic fibres and steel wires, it controls the shape of the tyre, how it deflects and flexes and the temperature it runs at.

A modern radial tyre. Michelin use special Delta construction for stability.

Typical road construction. Tread pattern is optimised for water clearance, ensuring grip in wet and dry conditions

A radial tyre showing the different plies.

Bias belted tyre.

Buying, choosing & fitting

Rear tyres usually wear out before fronts because that's where all the power is transmitted. Don't be tempted to mix and match tyre types or use one from a different manufacturer, though. They're designed and tested in pairs. If your tyres are tubed, fit a new inner tube too. Some radials can be fitted with tubes, but check with the manufacturer's recommendations. And always fit tyres of the correct load and speed ratings for your bike.

Don't buy oversize (that's wider) tyres for your bike thinking they'll give more grip. They won't, and there could be clearance problems with the swingarm or other chassis components, which will upset the handling. Likewise, an undersize tyre will have too flat a profile when fitted.

The Haynes workshop manual for your bike gives instructions on changing tyres, but if you don't feel up to the job, or your tyres are tubeless and you don't have access to a compressed air line, you might want to entrust the job to a tyre fitter. Tyres are directional, and the direction of rotation is indicated by an arrow on the sidewall. They must be fitted the right way round.

It's a good idea to have new valves fitted to the rims when having new tubeless tyres fitted, since the rubber bodies can harden and perish. Short valve stems minimise the problems of centrifugal force described in the first part of this chapter.

Some makes of tyres have coloured dots to indicate the lightest part of the tyre and the fitter must position this adjacent to the valve.

Tyre mounting lubricant or soapy water is used to clean the bead and help it seal. With the stem core of the valve removed, the tyre is inflated to about 50psi until the bead seats. The core is then refitted and the tyre inflated to operating pressure. Control lines concentric with the bead show if the tyre is evenly seated to the bead. If not, the tyre is deflated and the process repeated.

The wheel is then balanced, stick-on weights being put opposite the point the tyre always stops at until the wheel stops randomly when spun. Unbalanced wheels upset handling and tyre wear is accelerated.

Puncture repair with mushroom type plugs is possible on some tubeless tyres, depending on the severity of the hole. Puncture repair is not possible when the damage is on the sidewall rather than the tread. Different countries have different regulations, and manufacturers make their own recommendations. For safety reasons, these are best adhered to. Don't be tempted to patch punctured tubes – use new ones instead. Tubed tyre punctures, where fixable, should be repaired by vulcanisation to prevent moisture from attacking the carcass.

New tyres should be run-in for the first 100 miles or so. The tread of new tyres is smooth and therefore slippy. Running-in takes that top layer off. So no heavy braking, hard acceleration or cornering until the tyres are broken in.

If in doubt, hammer it out, or in. Tyre changer puts the rear spindle back in.

Wheel balancing is essential, especially for the front tyre. A good fitter will use a dynamic machine to do this for you.

Engine **types**

There are plenty of engine configurations in current production, but they all work in one of two ways – as two-strokes and four-strokes. The strokes refer to the number of times the piston moves up and down the bore in each combustion cycle. And that tells you a lot about the characteristics of the engine and its mechanical make-up.

The four-stroke process in four easy steps; suck, squeeze, bang, blow. Also known as the Otto cycle. It's powered most bikes of the last 100 years.

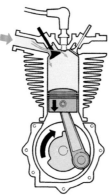

Induction: *as the piston descends the inlet valve opens, allowing the fuel/air mixture to be drawn directly into the combustion chamber.*

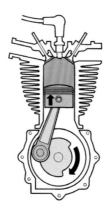

Compression: *the piston starts to ascend and the inlet valve closes. The mixture is compressed as the piston rises.*

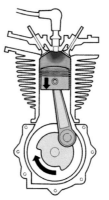

Ignition: *the spark plug ignites the compressed mixture, forcing the piston down the bore.*

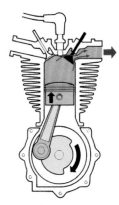

Exhaust: *the exhaust valve opens to allow the burnt gases to be expelled through the exhaust port as the piston rises.*

A combustion cycle consists of induction (air and fuel in), compression (squeezing the mixture), ignition (setting it alight) and exhaust (getting the spent gases out). This is the same no matter how many strokes an engine is. Helpfully, the stages are pretty self-explanatory.

Air and fuel are drawn into the combustion chamber during induction, squashed in compression, ignited and burnt during ignition (sometimes called power) and removed from the combustion chamber during exhaust. That's the process the engine has to go through in order to covert the chemical energy in petrol into something we can use to make our bike move.

There are several differences between two and four-stroke engines, but the most apparent is how they control the flow of gas in and out of the combustion chamber.

A four-stroke

The four-stroke gets its name because it takes four strokes to complete one combustion cycle. At the start of the cycle, the piston is at TDC (top dead centre – as far up the bore as it can travel), and the valves are shut. As the crankshaft turns, the piston drops down the bore and the inlet valve opens allowing fresh fuel and air mixture into the cylinder.

As the piston reaches BDC (bottom dead centre – as far down the bore as possible), the inlet valve closes, trapping the mixture in the cylinder. That is the induction stroke finished with.

As the crankshaft continues to rotate, it now starts to push the piston back up the bore towards TDC. Since all the valves are shut, sealing the cylinder, the air/fuel mixture has nowhere to go and gets compressed more and more until the piston is again at TDC. The piston has now done two strokes, one down the bore and one back up, and the crankshaft has turned through one revolution.

With the mixture squashed in the small space above the piston, it's ready to ignite – so the spark plug sparks and starts a fire in the mixture, causing it to expand rapidly and push forcibly on all the surfaces. As our piston is the only thing that can move, the high pressure in the cylinder pushes the piston back down the bore until it reaches BDC and can't be pushed any further. This is the end of the ignition/power stoke.

All that is required now is to empty the burnt gas from the cylinder. At this point, the exhaust valve opens and the high-pressure gas starts to make its way past the exhaust valve and into the exhaust pipe. This is helped by the piston, which is coming up the bore towards TDC, driving the gas out of the cylinder.

Once it reaches TDC, the exhaust valve closes and the inlet valve opens ready to start the next combustion cycle. In all the piston has moved in the bore four times and the crankshaft has rotated twice.

That's the simplified view of the four-stroke, although in fact the valves are timed so that the exhaust stays open briefly as the inlet opens to admit the fresh charge, the waste gases helping to draw in the next fresh mixture charge.

Two-strokes

A two-stroke goes through the same combustion cycle as a four-stroke, but in half the time. A two-stroke doesn't have valves in the top of the combustion chamber. Instead, it has holes (ports) in the cylinder wall, which are covered and uncovered by the piston as it rises and falls. By setting the ports at different levels, it's possible to cover and uncover them at the correct times in the induction and ignition cycles.

It's also important to know that two-strokes carry their lubrication in the air/fuel mixture, either pumped in from a separate tank to the crankcases to mix with the fuel or pre-mixed in the fuel tank. This mixture is held in the crankcase, underneath the piston before it enters the cylinder. The oil content in the mixture lubricates the crankshaft and con-rod bearings, and the rise and fall of the piston is used to pump the air/fuel mixture into the cylinder.

With the piston at BDC both the inlet and exhaust ports are uncovered, and fresh mixture is displaced into the cylinder through the inlet port. As the piston rises it first covers the inlet port, stopping any more mixture entering the cylinder and completing induction. As the piston rises further it also covers the exhaust port to seal the cylinder, and compression starts to take place.

The mixture is fully compressed when the piston reaches TDC, and in one movement the two-stroke has completed both induction and compression. The four-stroke's piston has to move twice to do this.

The spark plug now ignites the mixture to give us the power stroke. The piston is then forced back down the bore by the expanding gas until it uncovers the exhaust port. At this point the pressure of the burnt gas starts to escape into the exhaust pipe, completing both ignition/power and exhaust in one more stroke.

In all, the piston has gone up and down the bore once, but has completed all four parts of the combustion process. The crankshaft has gone round only once too. Rather than leave our piston waiting, we should explain that as it travels a little further down it uncovers the inlet port again, allowing fresh mixture to enter the cylinder.

At this point, exhaust gas will still be flowing out through the exhaust port while fresh mixture enters the cylinder via a process called scavenging. The big advantages of a two-stroke are that you get a power stroke for every crank revolution and there are fewer moving parts, which makes the engine cheaper and easier to build. The drawback is they aren't as efficient or economical as four-strokes.

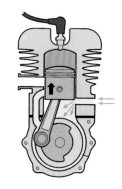

Induction of fresh mixture into crankcase and *compression* of existing mixture in combustion chamber.

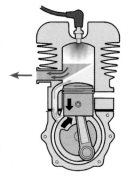

Ignition and exhaust of existing mixture in combustion chamber, and transfer of fresh mixture to combustion chamber.

Engine **layout**

As well as being two- or four-stroke, engines vary in their layout. The simplest is a single-cylinder engine, commonly found in anything from small commuter bikes to thumping supermotos. Normally the cylinder points straight up and sits on top of the crankcases and gearbox. You'll also find singles with their cylinder pointing forwards or at an angle (inclined). But singles are just the start of what's possible

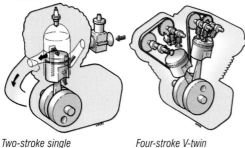

Two-stroke single　　　*Four-stroke V-twin*

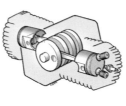

Four-stroke opposed twin

Two-stroke V-twin

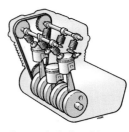

Four-stroke in-line triple

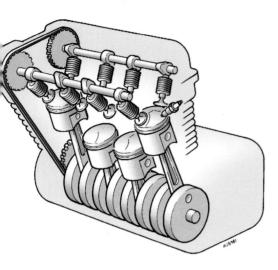

Four-stroke in-line four *Honda CBR1000RR is one of the finest examples of this layout.*

The next stage up from a single is to put two cylinders next to each other and make a parallel twin. This has several advantages because now there are two of everything. Two cylinders mean there is twice as much room to burn fuel, and gives the potential to have twice as many power strokes per crank revolution. But because we need only one crank and one gearbox, the engine doesn't have to be twice the physical size, which is an important factor as far as bikes are concerned.

As well as parallel twins, you'll also see 45°, 60° 70° and 90° V-twins, or opposed twins (BMW Boxers, for example) where the cylinders point in opposite directions. Each has slight advantages and disadvantages over the other but, in general, the most common twins at the moment are V-twins, made popular by Ducati and Harley Davidson.

The engine layout you're most likely to see these days is the in-line four, which is essentially two parallel twins side by side, albeit with a co-joined crank. In-line fours can be found in capacities from 250cc to 1400cc and are widely used since they balance compactness with the ability to make large amounts of power. They also run smoothly because of their configuration and can rev higher, which makes them easy to tune and good for everyday riding. Vibration is quite a big concern on singles and parallel twins. This problem is normally reduced with balancer shafts, although with the right engine layout these are almost unnecessary.

Finally, there are a collection of other configurations such as V4s, used by Honda in its VFR sports-tourer range and race bikes, V6s, opposed fours, triples and even in-line sixes, although you won't see many of those around. We're likely to see a host of new configurations in the future as technology developed in GP racing makes its way into road bikes. These could include V5s and V3s, which are being raced or developed at the moment.

Racing has always improved the breed, and soon we'll be taking our pleasure on a new class of thoroughbred.

Four-stroke V4 *is a Honda favourite, this is a VFR800F.*

Four-stroke single *easiest and cheapest four-stroke to manufacture for reliable performance.*

Four-stroke parallel twin *backbone of the old British bike industry, finds favour in OHC form today.*

Transmission

All the power being generated by your engine has to find its way to the back wheel as efficiently as possible. And that's the job of the transmission or drive train. There are four main elements here – primary drive, clutch, gearbox and final drive.

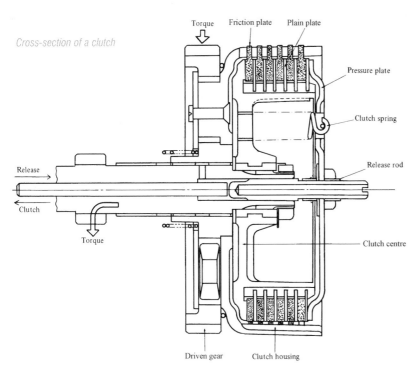

Cross-section of a clutch

Labels on diagram: Torque, Friction plate, Plain plate, Pressure plate, Clutch spring, Release rod, Release, Clutch, Torque, Clutch centre, Driven gear, Clutch housing

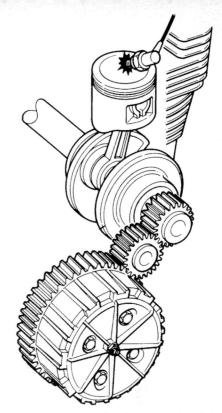

How the piston and crank connect with the clutch via the primary drive.

Every powered two-wheeler needs the four main transmission elements to move forward, although these vary in type and detail from bike to bike. There's a further main sub-division of transmission types – manual and automatic. Manual transmission is the most common system for motorcycles, although some bike manufacturers, most notably Guzzi and Honda, have played around with automatic transmission in the past. Automatic transmission is the preserve of mopeds and scooters, although some of these sport manual systems.

Primary drive

This is the link between the crankshaft – spinning merrily round propelled by the con-rods and pistons – and the clutch. The connection is usually achieved either by chain or belt, or more commonly these days, gear. To propel machine and rider forward, especially from standstill and at low engine speeds, we need plenty of torque – the twisting force that ultimately manifests itself at the back wheel.

The primary drive is the first stage in generating sufficient torque to get the bike moving. A typical arrangement is a smaller gear (the input or drive gear) on the end of the crank driving (by gear, chain or belt) a larger gear (the driven or output gear), around the clutch housing. The ratios of these gears dictate by how much the torque at the crank is multiplied. If the input gear has half the number of teeth of the output gear, the output gear turns at half the speed and doubles the torque of the input gear. If the output has three times the teeth, it turns at a third of the speed of the input and produces three times the torque, and so on.

The process of torque multiplication and reduction continues throughout the drive train to deliver the optimum amount of torque for what the rider wants the bike to do.

Clutch

The clutch's job is to disconnect the running engine from the gearbox and final drive. If it wasn't there, the engine would have to be stopped every time the bike pulled up. It also allows drive to be disengaged so you can change gear without crashing through the gearbox and stressing the components. In order to do this smoothly, it has to work progressively via the rider's input to the handlebar lever.

There are different types of clutch around, but they all have one thing in common – they work through friction.

Most manual clutches found on bikes these days consist of a drum or outer driven by the primary, as described above, mounted on the gearbox's input shaft. This is free to turn independently of the input shaft when the clutch is disengaged. The clutch centre is splined to the input shaft. When it turns, the gearbox turns. The drum and the centre are linked by a number of plates, plain steel and friction, which again are steel, but also have inserts of friction material.

The friction plates have teeth on their outer diameter which locate in the drum, and the plain ones have teeth that locate with the clutch centre. The clutch pressure plate pulls the lot together using the clutch springs, and the friction between the sets of plates lets the engine drive the gearbox. When the clutch lever is pulled in, the pressure plate is moved slightly away from the plates, which means there is insufficient friction for the engine to drive the gearbox.

Wet multi-plate clutches are the most common set-up. 'Wet' means the plates run in oil to keep them cool and 'multi-plate' means there is more than one set of plates. The use of numerous plates allows the diameter of the clutch to be kept small, but there is still a sufficient area of friction material to handle the torque generated without clutch slip.

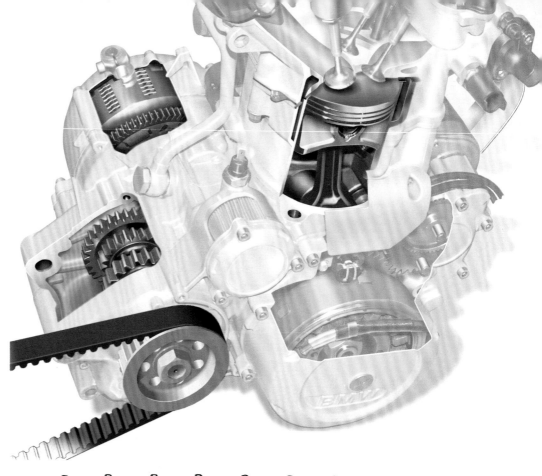

BMW's F650 shows the crank, primary drive, gearbox interface, although the belt final drive is unusual.

Clutch drum driven by primary gears.

Clutch centre connects to gearbox.

Clutch plates alternating plain and friction plates. Friction plates spin with the engine, so when pressed against plain plates, spin the gearbox.

Pressure plate applies and releases pressure on friction plates.

Some designs use single or double-plate clutches – for example, BMW Boxers and Guzzis where the crankshaft is in line with the frame, the clutch mounted on the end of the crank and running at engine speed. These plates are larger in diameter and have to run dry to deal with the torque. As they run at engine speed, torque multiplication takes place elsewhere in the drive train.

Smaller bikes, such as mopeds and scooters, that have automatic transmission run a different type of clutch. Some are governed by centrifugal force, where as the revs rise, shoes like those in a brake drum are thrust into contact with a clutch outer, taking up drive. The other type is called ball and ramp, where as engine speed rises and the clutch outer rotates faster, ball bearings acting on angled ramps against the pressure plate rise on the ramps to engage drive. This type of clutch is very similar to the wet multi-plate units found on bigger bikes.

Manual clutch operation can be by cable or hydraulic. Hydraulic systems are usually found only on high-end sports machines. They provide a lighter action than cable, for the same reasons that hydraulic brakes have more feel and force than cable systems.

Gearbox

The gearbox's job is as simple as its parts look complex. It's there to make the engine turn at a reasonable speed whatever the desired road speed. A side-effect of this is that it dictates the number of powerstrokes needed during each revolution of the rear wheel, as dictated by the need to accelerate machine and rider from rest or low speed.

As internal combustion engines make usable power in only very narrow power bands, gearboxes containing the correct ratios are required to make the most of what is there and keep the powerband as wide as possible. Let's say you're on a sportsbike, accelerating hard in second towards 10,000rpm. Clearly you wouldn't want the rear wheel spinning at the same rate as the engine – you'd almost be clear for take-off. Instead, you want the right amount of torque, as set by the manufacturer getting its torque multiplication sums right, to provide linear acceleration until it's time for the next gearshift. If the ratios are right (and they should be if the manufacturer has been attentive), the rev counter drops to the bottom of the power band when you change gear. Then it rises again as you open the throttle, until you run out of gears, power and, ultimately, road.

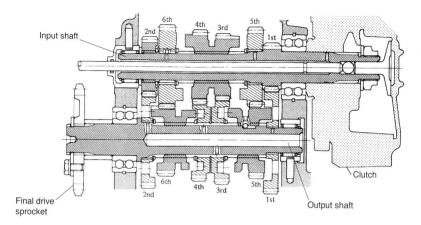

Input shaft

6th
4th
2nd
3rd
5th
1st

Here's how it all hangs together in a typical constant mesh, six-speed motorcycle gearbox.

Clutch

Final drive sprocket

6th
2nd
4th
3rd
5th
1st

Output shaft

Ratios on road bikes are chosen for flexibility rather than outright performance. By contrast, race bike ratios are chosen to work in extremely narrow power bands at the top of the rev range. Hence, first gear on a race bike makes it hard to pull away from the lights without slipping the clutch – but then race bikes only have to pull away from standstill once per outing, where a road bike has to do it many times. That's why it's equipped with higher ratios (lower gears) at the bottom of the 'box.

Gearboxes contain a number of gear pairs, usually between four and six. The principles of torque multiplication apply here too, first gear being a small cog on the input shaft driving a much larger one on the output shaft. At the other end of the scale, top gear consists of a gear on the input shaft that is the same size or sometimes larger than the one on the output. This ensures that there's plenty of thrust in the lower gears for acceleration, yet comfortable cruising in the higher ones with, power permitting, enough oomph for overtaking and so on. Usually gears are in constant mesh, whether they are driving or being driven or not, and slide and engage on their respective shafts as they're selected by the gear shift, which moves the relevant pair of gears together on the shafts.

Final drive

The most common final drive system in current use is chain and sprockets, a small front and larger rear linked by a roller chain. There's also the less common belt type, as found on Harley-Davidsons, for example. As the section on chain care explains, the conventional chain and sprocket arrangement is very susceptible to road dirt and the elements, so regular maintenance is essential to slow the rate of the inevitible wear of both chain and sprockets.

Some bikes use shaft-drive systems. These are relatively low-maintenance and have better longevity than chains and sprockets, but are heavy, adding to unsprung weight, and don't transfer power as efficiently as chains. It's also much harder to change final drive ratios, should you wish to. What's more, there's the problem of torque reaction on a trailing throttle or under hard acceleration as the system struggles to deal with its own backlash between the gear teeth or the sudden take-up of drive. And as chains and sprockets are cheaper to manufacture than shafts, it's likely that manufacturers will stick with those for the foreseeable future.

A BMW F650's final belt drive. Is this the way forward, or have rumours of the chain's demise been greatly exaggerated?

Tuning four-strokes

Tuning engines can mean many different things. In some ways, a service is a form of tuning because you adjust components to their optimum settings and replace parts as required. You're effectively tuning the engine to behave as it did when it was new. To most people, though, tuning is about more performance. They want their bike to go faster, and for that the engine needs to make more power and torque.

Engines basically convert the chemical energy in petrol into usable power and torque. So it makes sense that the more petrol an engine can burn, the more power and torque you can get out of it. This is true to a point, but you can't just shove in more fuel, because there won't be enough air to burn it properly unless that side of the induction process is addressed. And even if there is sufficient air, the engine may not make more power if it burns inefficiently, or loses the extra power through friction.

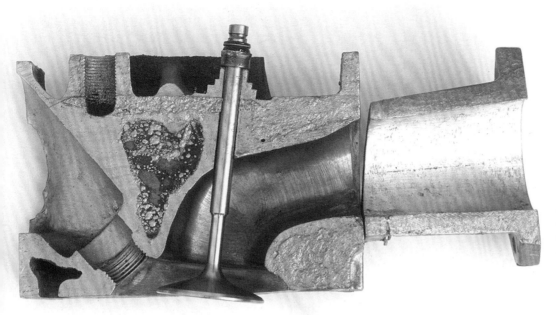

An inlet tract and valve. This is where it all begins, and things have to be right here for your engine to make optimum power.

So tuning can almost be summed up as burning more fuel, extracting energy more completely and losing less of whatever the motor produces. First, look at what's stopping the engine getting that air and fuel in, and make them more efficient. For getting air/fuel into and out of the engine, this means looking at the airbox and filters, carbs or throttle bodies, inlet and exhaust tracts in the cylinder head, valves, camshafts and exhaust system.

Don't charge straight in and cut bits out of the cylinder head hoping to improve flow. Modern computer-designed cylinder heads are exceedingly good already, and it's easier to make them worse rather than better. Most people start by replacing the standard air filter since these are generally quite restrictive. By fitting a filter that can flow air more easily, you've already reduced one of the restrictions – and you've done it without great expense. You also risk making the mixture dangerously lean unless the issue of fuel supply is also addressed.

As the cylinder head is one of the biggest factors controlling how well an engine can breathe, it makes sense to tune it. But this should really be left to professionals, who have the experience to know what works and why. Most amateurs will dive in, make all the ports larger and change the shape to something they think looks nice. But when they run the engine it makes less power. Bigger isn't always best, and once you've ground metal out it's hard to put it back in again.

Perhaps one of the most effective forms of tuning for road bikes is blueprinting. The motivation of blueprinting an engine isn't just to get more performance, although that is invariably a by-product of it. Blueprinting is, as the name suggests, modifying an engine until it is exactly as the original designer's blueprint intended, before the accountants and processes that rule mass-production took over.

Although mass-production means we get our bikes cheaper, it also means there are power-sapping production tolerances to be met. The first bike off the production line might be

spot-on, but 500 bikes later the bits in the milling machines will be worn. Of course they're replaced as required but manufacturers still build to tolerances, which means you might get one bike exactly right but another where those key machine tools were at the limit.

We see the results of this most often on the dyno. It's possible to test two bikes of the same age, make and model but see different results (as much as 15–20 per cent) and most of this is down to production tolerances.

When an engine is blueprinted it's stripped down to the individual components and each is measured and weighed to make sure it matches the others. Pistons, for example, will be machined so they all weigh the same, eliminating strain on the crank and con-rods, reducing vibration and giving smoother power delivery. They will also be machined to give the same amount of valve-to-piston clearance in all the cylinders.

This principle is applied throughout the engine until you end up with a perfect engine. It generally makes more power because the tolerances are correct, should be more reliable because it's only tuned to its design spec and is certainly nicer to use.

The next step usually involves component lightening, polishing and other practices of the tuner's esoteric art.

A two-stroke may have fewer moving parts, in that there are no valves and camshafts to worry about, but blueprinting works here too. The main concern is still how the mixture gets in and out of the engine, and how quickly.

Tuning can become extreme, however. And the more power you have, the harder – and more expensive – it becomes to get even more. There will also come a point when your engine becomes so focused it's not very practical or pleasant to ride on the road. It might only make useable power at the top of the rev range and that's no good for road riding. A broad spread through the rev range is best for roadsters. For this reason, it's important to know what you want to achieve through tuning, and why, before you start.

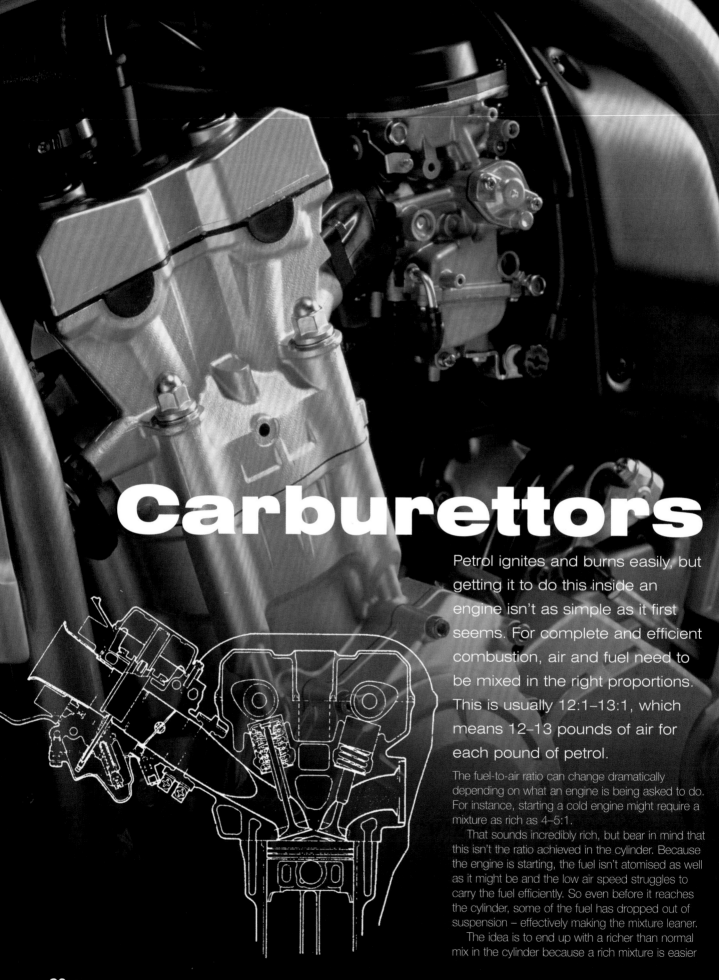

Carburettors

Petrol ignites and burns easily, but getting it to do this inside an engine isn't as simple as it first seems. For complete and efficient combustion, air and fuel need to be mixed in the right proportions. This is usually 12:1–13:1, which means 12–13 pounds of air for each pound of petrol.

The fuel-to-air ratio can change dramatically depending on what an engine is being asked to do. For instance, starting a cold engine might require a mixture as rich as 4–5:1.

That sounds incredibly rich, but bear in mind that this isn't the ratio achieved in the cylinder. Because the engine is starting, the fuel isn't atomised as well as it might be and the low air speed struggles to carry the fuel efficiently. So even before it reaches the cylinder, some of the fuel has dropped out of suspension – effectively making the mixture leaner.

The idea is to end up with a richer than normal mix in the cylinder because a rich mixture is easier to ignite – and that makes starting easier. In contrast, a cruising ratio might be as lean as 18:1.

So much for mixture proportions, but how does a carburettor actually work? Carbs work because they have something called a venturi. This is essentially a restriction where the passage through the carburettor narrows, then opens up again. As air passes through the venturi it drops in pressure, and it is this differential which can be utilised.

Fuel from your tank flows into the carbs and is held in the float-bowl, where it waits until something causes it to do otherwise. In this case, the otherwise is low pressure in the venturi, which is connected to the float-bowl by a passage. Although it's only at atmospheric pressure, the air in the float-bowl is relatively high compared to the venturi. This drives fuel up the passage, through the main jet into an emulsion tube and finally into the air stream, where it is broken down into tiny droplets that are carried into the combustion chamber by the air.

The most common type of carburettor fitted to bikes is the CV (constant velocity) carb. This is a clever device that controls the flow of air through the venturi to help deliver the correct amount of fuel, regardless of how open or shut the throttle plate is, by maintaining the correct pressure in the venturi.

In effect, the rider doesn't directly control the slide in the carb. Instead, the carb monitors the vacuum in the inlet tract, which is controlled by the rider using the throttle plate, and uses this to operate a vacuum slide. The greater the vacuum the more the slide lifts. It sounds complicated but isn't really. It's just a system to help stop the engine bogging-down.

A slide, or flat-slide, carb works in the same way, but the throttle directly opens and closes the slide in the venturi. In effect you control the velocity of air, and therefore fuel.

It's possible to get more power using a flat-slide carb because there is less clutter in the inlet tract when the throttle is wide open. But the drawback is that the rider must have a good understanding of what the engine requires and the necessary skill to operate the throttle accordingly.

You can't just open the throttle with a flat-slide carb to accelerate – especially from low to mid-revs. Because the engine isn't revving very fast, the velocity of air through the carb is relatively slow. Suddenly opening the slide effectively increases the diameter of the venturi, reducing its effectiveness, and also lowers the vacuum in the inlet tract.

This means there isn't enough pressure differential to move enough fuel through the carb and not enough velocity to carry it efficiently to the cylinder. The engine will become starved of fuel and bog. In some cases the engine will recover, but if the revs continue to drop and the throttle remains wide open, the revs fall and the problem gets worse.

CV carbs let the engine run far more smoothly than slide carbs because they avoid this. And they also allow you to ride the bike without worrying about the throttle and fuelling demands of the engine.

A typical bank of CV carbs from an in-line four.

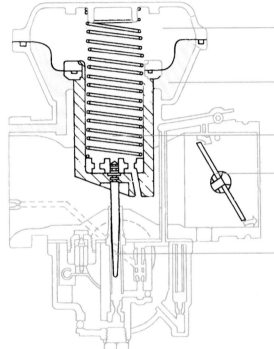

Constant velocity (CV) carburettor

Air is routed up into the vacuum chamber via a hole in the base of the piston.

Air at atmospheric pressure fills the area below the diaphragm.

Return spring helps to stabilise the piston.

Throttle as the throttle is opened, low pressure is created in the vacuum chamber and the piston begins to rise.

Needle the piston has a tapered needle attached which blocks the fuel flow. As it is lifted, petrol is drawn up by the low pressure.

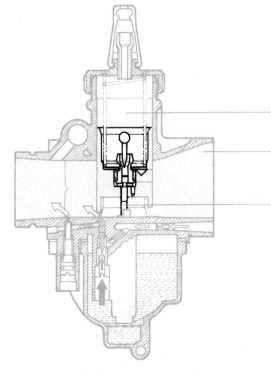

Slide Carburettor

Piston is directly controlled by the twist grip.

Air pressure drops as the piston is lifted and more air flows.

Needle the piston has a tapered needle attached which blocks the fuel flow. As it is lifted petrol is drawn up by the low pressure.

Carburettor **tuning**

Tuning carburettors and actually improving their performance is a true black art, especially as they have been around for so long and most things have been tried already. So the first thing to consider is what exactly you are trying to do.

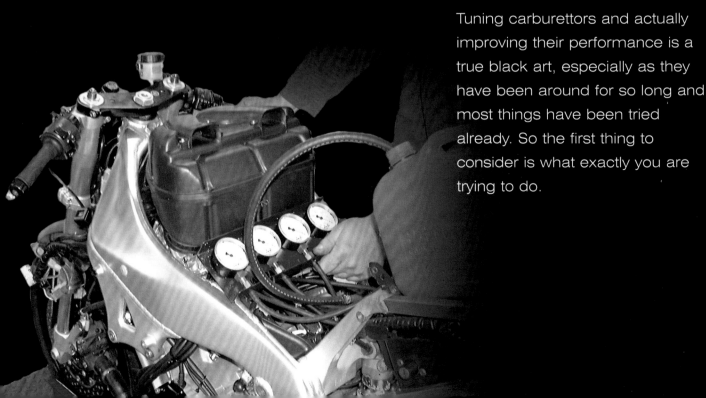

There are many reasons to fiddle with a carburettor. It might be to get rid of that annoying flat-spot at 5000rpm or to make the engine run smoother. Or you may have fitted a new exhaust with different flow characteristics. Whatever it is, chances are it'll be more complicated than you think.

However, there are a few things you can do. The most common alteration to carbs is to balance or synchronise them, assuming there is more than one carb, that is. Balancing the carbs ensures they are all drawing the same amount of air and fuel – so you get the same performance and response from each cylinder. Once adjusted correctly, the power delivery will definitely feel smoother. Unbalanced carbs can even lead to a degree of vibration that feels like serious engine problems.

Balancing is done by connecting vacuum gauges to the inlet tracts and adjusting the synchronisation screws on the carbs. This a very fine way of adjusting the throttle plate so the vacuum in the inlet tracts are the same. Ideally, the vacuum levels of the carbs will match, although sometimes carbs are balanced as pairs, with the inner and outer pairs on a four-cylinder machine running differently. Check your manual if unsure.

It's also important to keep carbs clean – both internally and externally. Dirt tends to accumulate on carbs because of the residue that invariably forms on them. In time, this greasy paste can cause problems and certainly doesn't make it easy to work on or even check the condition of carbs. Careful use of a degreaser is normally enough to keep them clean.

Cleaning carbs internally needs to be done rarely, but if a bike has been stored with fuel in the carbs, it can evaporate from the system and leave a gummy residue, which blocks jets. In this case, the carb should be stripped and cleaned or at least have some aerosol carb cleaner run through it.

It's not so common now, but people used to scrap their existing carbs in favour of ones with bigger throats. The logic is that if more mixture can get into the engine, it'll make more power. While there is a hint of truth about this, it isn't that simple.

As we mentioned previously, carbs mix fuel relative to the vacuum in their venturi. As you get a lower pressure with a smaller venturi, so the reverse is true. Although you increase the flow potential of the engine by fitting bigger carbs, what you normally get is awful fuelling because they're unable thoroughly to mix the correct amount of fuel.

In some ways, a smaller bore carburettor is better for road use because it will improve the mid-range response of the engine. Manufacturers often use this trick when they make less extreme versions of their bikes. Yamaha did this when it fitted the R1 engine into the Fazer 1000.

To set a carb up properly, it's wise to measure the air/fuel ratio in the exhaust. Most dyno houses have this equipment and can run the bike to check that the mixture isn't too rich or lean. To affect the overall ratio of the bike it's necessary to change the main jet. The bigger the hole in it, the greater the flow of fuel and so the richer the mixture becomes.

There are other adjustments too. In most cases, it's possible to 'lift the needle'. This simply means adjusting the height of the needle relative to the slide. Most adjustable needles have three or four grooves at the top, and by moving a clip to different grooves you can raise or lower the needle. This has the effect of allowing more or less fuel to flow through the needle jet for a given throttle opening.

Adjustable needle
The locating circlip can be raised or lowered on the needle to provide fine tuning.

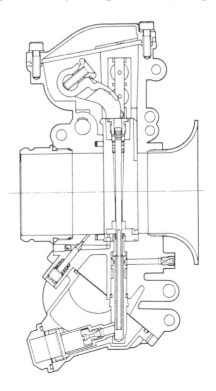

Flat-Slide Carburettor
Mikuni TDMR40, supplied with the Suzuki GSX-R750W race kit. Note angled float bowl and offset main jet, designed to keep the carburettor compact and let it operate at a steep downdraught angle. (Suzuki)

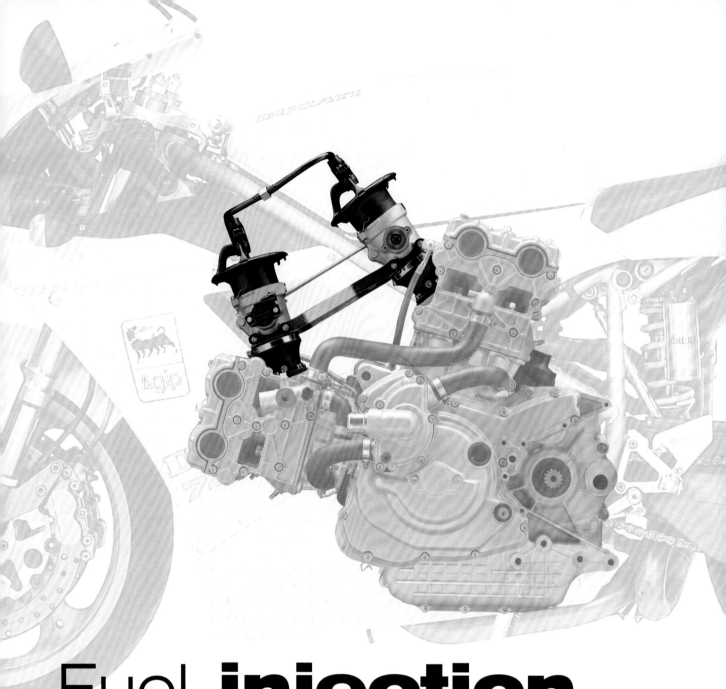

Fuel **injection**

Fuel injection A pair of injectors look huge atop the heads of this Ducati 748. But the Italian firm have realised the potency and efficiency of effective injection.

Despite carburettors being refined over many years to a point where they're taken for granted, the world moves on – and in the direction of fuel injection. Fuel injection is not a new technology. In fact, it's been around in cars for so long even

the most basic models have it. Every year more and more motorcycles are being fitted with fuel injection. The once common complaint of glitchy delivery is heard less often as manufacturers refine their systems.

Honda injection system from the RC45. More and more sportsbikes feature injection.

Fuel Injector

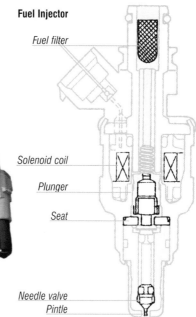

Fuel filter

Solenoid coil

Plunger

Seat

Needle valve
Pintle

Inside an injector. The actual engineering looks simple, but injection requires complex electronics to control it effectively.

A fuel injection system is essentially made up of one or more injectors, a number of sensors and a control unit. Unlike carburettors, which are governed by the laws of physics and therefore know what to do intrinsically, a fuel injection system has to be told. For this reason, a fuel-injected bike is covered in sensors.

You might think a cylinder with a displacement of 250cc will suck in a quarter of a litre of air with each induction stroke, but this is not quite the case. Even with the throttle wide open, most engines only fill their cylinders between 80 and 95 per cent of their maximum capacity because there's so little time to do it and so many restrictions. The point at which an engine most effectively fills its cylinders will be when peak torque occurs.

Because the engine doesn't always draw in the same amount of air, the most important thing the ECU (electronic control unit) needs to know is how fast the engine is revving and how far open the throttle is. Using this information, and knowing roughly how well the engine will fill its cylinder under those conditions, it sets off to a library stored in its memory to find out how much fuel to inject.

Unfortunately, that is not enough. If the engine is being started from cold, it needs a rich mixture, so engine temperature needs checking. The system also needs to know the air pressure – higher pressure means denser air, and that requires more fuel to get the correct ratio. Remember, the ratio is by weight, not volume.

As if working out the correct amount of fuel to inject wasn't hard enough, the ECU also has to deliver precisely that amount – and this can be a job in itself. When you turn the key on an injected bike, you'll hear a fuel pump whirr into life. This pumps fuel into a rail connected to the injectors, effectively making them little taps. When an injector opens, fuel flows from the rail into the engine.

The amount of fuel flowing depends on three things: the flow rate of the injector; the amount of time it's open; and the flow rate from the pump. The injector's rating remains the same but the open time and pressure both vary, and these need to be taken into account too.

The list of information required by the ECU goes on, and the more there is, the better the end result will be. Armed with all the information, the ECU determines how long it needs to open each injector to deliver the required fuel. It then sends a timed signal to the injector, which opens and closes a small nozzle in its end. The opening time is a matter of milliseconds.

This is where injectors better carbs, though. By forcing fuel through a nozzle under pressure, the fuel is equally atomised in all conditions. And the smaller the fuel droplets are, the better they can mix with the air. End result: more efficiency and power.

For maximum performance, some bikes have more than one injector per cylinder. The extra injector is normally fitted at the mouth of the inlet tract and only kicks in at high revs. One advantage of this system is that the injected fuel is more evenly spread through the inlet charge, which gives a better burn and more performance.

A single injector, capable of supplying enough fuel at high revs, would only have to open very briefly at lower revs, concentrating the fuel in a portion of the intake air. An injector with a smaller capacity would have to stay open longer to deliver the same amount of fuel, and in that time more air would pass by it.

Electronics also bring a greater degree of control. Most bikes reference different fuel maps depending on what gear they're in. Fuel injection allows manufacturers to control things down to the very last detail, and that means bikes can respond better, whatever our needs.

Exhaust systems

Exhaust systems aren't just there to keep the noise down. In fact, the only reason engines have silencers fitted at all is because legislation says they must – being quiet doesn't improve performance... But even without this legislation, bikes would still have exhaust pipes of some sort because they are just as responsible for engine performance as any other part.

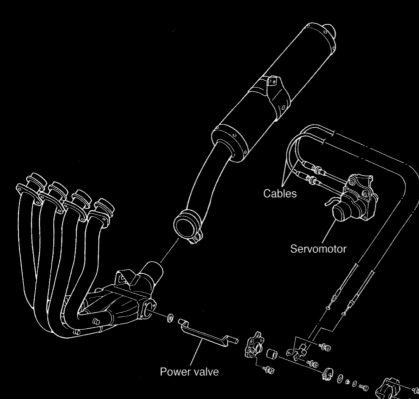

Yamaha exhaust system features that company's famous EXUP valve which helps optimise power delivery.

Cables

Servomotor

Power valve

Modern exhaust systems are built from a number of materials. Low-performance or economy bikes still tend towards steel exhaust systems because they're cheap and functional. High-performance bikes use more exotic lightweight materials, such as titanium, and carbon fibre. This has little to no effect on engine power but a large impact on your wallet. They're actually more about saving weight than anything else.

The design of modern sportbike exhausts has come a long way since the late 1990s, and a lot of work goes into them. For starters, they have to be the right bore. In many ways, you'd think a bigger bore pipe would be best because it can flow more gas, but this isn't always the case.

A big-bore pipe helps an engine make good top-end power because it can flow large amounts of gas quickly. However, a smaller bore pipe can give a useful boost to low- and mid-range power by keeping the gas velocity up, which helps it to pull burnt gas from the cylinder.

As well as gas flow, pressure waves can be used in exhaust systems, and are absolutely crucial in two-strokes. These pulses are caused by the flow of gas and by the valves opening and closing. When the exhaust valve closes, it sends a high-pressure wave down the exhaust pipe and part of the energy in the wave will be reflected as a negative wave back down the pipe when it reaches the end. Timed correctly, this negative wave will

arrive just as the valve opens and encourage the gas in the cylinder to start moving. This effect only works at certain points in the rev range.

The formation of the pipes has an effect on power too. Some four-cylinder bikes have a 4-2-1, where the four header pipes converge into two pairs, before converging again into a single pipe. Others have a 4-1. There are advantages to each. A 4-2-1 system promotes mid-range power but isn't as efficient at high revs. The 4-1 system is the opposite, boosting top end but sacrificing some mid-range.

Power valves are also fairly common. They can be found in the ports of two-stroke motors and in the exhausts of four-strokes. In each case, they fool the engine into thinking that it has the best of both worlds. They do this by altering the exhaust port timing, the tuned length of the exhaust pipe or the configuration. Either way, the idea is to use the exhaust gas to help get more gas out of the cylinder and so more fresh mixture in.

Two-strokes are perhaps more responsive to the effects of exhaust pipes. You only have to look at their swoopy shapes and bulges to see that a lot of thought goes into them. In general, they aim to return a low-pressure wave at the exhaust port as it opens and a high-pressure wave just before it shuts. This makes a big difference to the scavenging ability of the engine, and can enhance and move the powerband.

Underseat exhaust
Many modern sportsbikes have MotoGP-style underseat exhausts. These help with mass centralisation, moving as much weight as possible to the centre of the bike to optimise handling. Noise limits make it tricky for designers to fit them to road bikes while continuing to extract optimum power, but many manufacturers have succeeded.

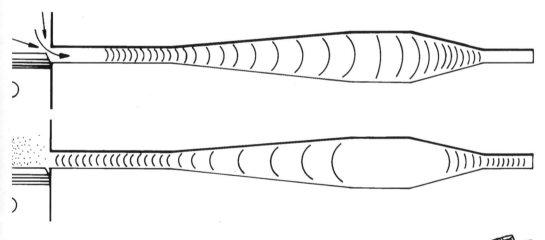

Two-stroke expansion chamber exhaust system
Spent gases rush out as a high-pressure wave, gradually expanding and losing velocity until reaching the reversed cone. Gases are compressed by the reverse cone and a proportion returns as a reverse pulse. This creates high pressure at the exhaust port, stopping fresh mixture escaping down the exhaust.

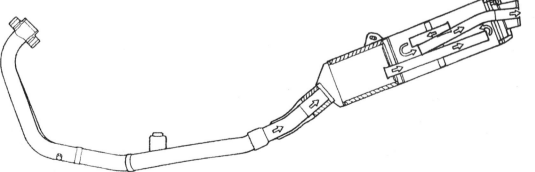

Four-stroke exhaust
System of internal baffles keeps noise down, hopefully not sacrificing too much power.

Race &
performance
exhausts

We've already looked at standard exhaust systems and seen that reducing noise isn't really what they are there for. So when tuning bikes, it makes sense to get rid of the noise restrictions, as these normally work by forcing the exhaust gas back and forth through a series of noise deadening chambers – and that's quite restrictive.

Yoshimura race can
There are dozens of can manufacturers, Yoshimura is one of the longest established.

Harris carbon can
Carbon fibre is a popular material for exhaust cans. And extremely fashionable too.

Yoshimura Tri-oval
Another offering from the celebrated tuning firm. Slimline form gives plenty of ground clearance.

Bike exhaust systems are not made in one piece, which allows just the silencer to be replaced without touching the rest of the system. This is a quick and simple modification, and it's quite cheap too. The standard silencers are normally replaced with slip-on race cans. The slip-on refers to their ease of fitment and the race bit simply means they're not road legal.

In almost all cases, the exhaust gas is free to travel straight through the centre of the can because it does away with the sound chambers. The can is lined with a perforated tube and sound deadening material, though, so it does cut down noise a little bit. Over time, its ability to do this will reduce and eventually it'll need repacking.

By increasing the ability of gas to flow through the exhaust system, it can move faster and in larger amounts. As far as the engine is concerned, this means it can rev more easily because it does not have to push gas through the exhaust system. But there are other implications.

With less pressure in the exhaust, it's easier for burnt gases in the combustion chamber to get out. And the faster that happens, the quicker fresh mixture can be drawn in to replace it. The result is more power, although it's wise to check the bike's fuelling on a rolling road, because fitting an end-can might cause the engine to run lean.

One trade-off might be a slight loss of mid-range power. As new mixture is drawn into the combustion chamber, it can get sucked straight out of the exhaust port.

Race cans flow more gas, so the fuel system must also supply more fuel to keep the correct mixture. This is only a serious problem if the mixture becomes dangerously lean and happens to do so in the type of conditions in which you often ride – say, 7000rpm with part-throttle. Having the bike set-up on a dyno will reveal any potential problems and also allow the fuelling to be optimised.

As well as replacing the end-can, people often replace the rest of the exhaust system. In the past, they did this because standard systems were built to a price and to give good results over a broad rev-range. By fitting after-market systems, people could pay for performance boosting features that increased engine performance in one area – usually top-end power for racing.

Now, though, many standard high-performance systems already come with features such as tapered header and crossover pipes. Both these features are designed to make best use of pressure waves and pulses travelling backwards and forwards through the exhaust. As with two-stroke exhausts, they're timed to reflect low-pressure waves on to the back of the exhaust valves just before they open, encouraging flow. A well-designed full-system can increase power by 3–10bhp.

Although it's always nice to increase the performance of your bike, there can be drawbacks. Some systems and even end-cans mean you have to remove a centre stand. If this is something you use all the time, it's worth searching around to find a system that lets you retain this.

It is also worth remembering that most race cans and full-systems aren't road legal. So as well as being louder and drawing more attention to yourself, you might end up in trouble with the law.

It should be possible to fit a full system and end-can yourself with only a few tools. Generally, the system will fix to the exhaust ports with two Allen bolts per cylinder, have a couple of brackets under the engine and finally be supported by a bracket or clamp on the end-can. It's important to get a good seal on any joints since gas leaks will reduce performance slightly, but more annoyingly, cause the bike to back fire on a shut throttle. Use an exhaust joint sealer and check for leaks once fitted.

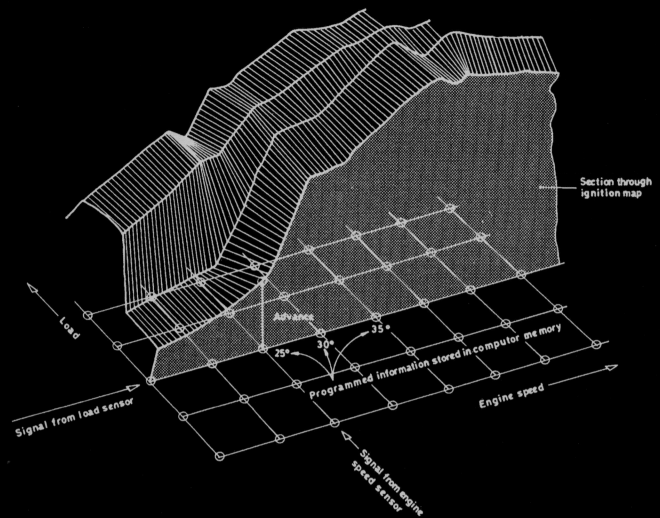

Section through ignition map

Load

Advance

Signal from load sensor

25°   30°   35°

Programmed information stored in computor memory

Signal from engine speed sensor

Engine speed

Electronic **C**ontrol **U**nits & **ignition**

The majority of bikes now have a small black box tucked away somewhere under the plastics – it's the ECU (electronic control unit). These seemingly impregnable boxes control most of the things going on in the engine. But that may not be as much as you think. At most, an ECU governs the fuel injection, ignition timing and sometimes a power valve or two.

Dynojet Power Commander
This clever device allows the info going to and from the ECU to be manipulated to optimise fuelling and/or ignition.

Schematic of a typical modern motorcycle system. At its heart lies the electronic control unit which collects information from sensors all over the bike then tells the key components what to do.

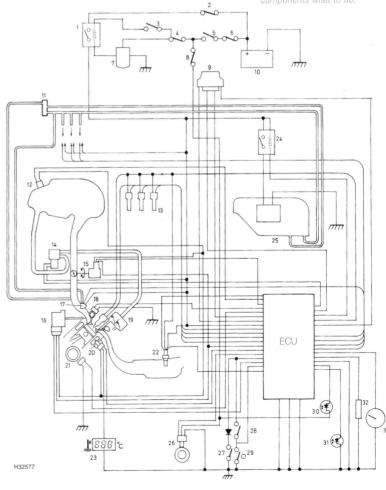

So why have them? Because they're more versatile and accurate than mechanical systems, that's why. They're also smaller, lighter and cheaper to produce.

Fuel injection is perhaps the biggest user of black boxes. We've already touched on carburettors and what a good job they do, despite the many conditions they have to work under. Fuel injection, on the other hand, is essentially dumb and has to be told what to do under each condition it might encounter. For this reason, it needs good, up-to-date information before it makes any decision.

The black box collects information from a number of sensors on the bike. These include throttle position, engine revs, crankshaft position, water temperature, air temperature and air pressure. Generally, more sensors mean the ECU can make a more accurate decision on how much fuel to inject. It then sends a signal to open and close the injector long enough to deliver that precise amount of fuel.

ECUs also control ignition timing. Again, to make the best decision possible, they need information. So at any time, the ECU will know what position the crankshaft is in and what demands are being made of the engine. It then references that information against a table stored in its memory and advances or retards the ignition as required.

In many ways, it's easier to tune bikes using the ECU than it is to do the same job manually. There are several devices available, such as Dynojet's Power Commander and Yoshimura's EMS, which plug into the bike's ECU and alter the signals. Doing this allows

**Four-stroke,
four-valve cylinder**

*A dramatic representation of
what happens inside a
four-stroke bike's cylinders.*

you to manipulate the information being sent to, or
from, the ECU. So you can control the fuelling and
ignition at almost any point in the rev range without
affecting anything else – something that's difficult to
do with carbs or mechanical ignitions. To set it up,
you just need someone with a dyno, load cell and
the necessary software and experience.

The potential to exploit black-box technology is
very exciting. Already we've seen how Suzuki used
it to good effect with its dual throttle-valve injector
bodies. The result is a virtual CV carb with injectors.

In the past, fuel-injected bikes suffered in similar
ways to flat-slide carbs (although to a lesser degree
because of the injectors), because the rider had
direct control over the throttle plate. With its GSX-R
series, Suzuki has incorporated a second throttle
valve controlled by the black box to maintain the
optimum intake velocity – a helping hand on the
throttle, if you like.

In theory, the same unit could also control
variable length inlet tracts to boost mid-range and
top-end power. Honda has already fitted traction
control to some of its bikes, but there's no reason
why this couldn't be extended to sporty models

too. And, with the correct sensors, you could even
end up with a bike that knows when it's raining and
switches to a softer fuel injection map for more
controllable delivery as well as turning on the
traction control system.

Ignition

The ignition is the system responsible for igniting
the air/fuel mixture in the combustion chamber. This
is more difficult than it first sounds, though. For
starters, the mixture has to be ignited at just the
right time to give maximum power, and in engines
this is measured in degrees of crank rotation before
or after the piston is at top dead centre (TDC), or
highest point.

It surprises many people to know that, in many
cases, the air/fuel mixture is actually lit *before* the
piston reaches the top of its stroke. They know that
when the mixture burns it expands and pushes
down on the piston, but what they forget is that the
mixture burns – it doesn't explode.

For this reason, the inertia of the crank is
enough for it to keep turning, despite the burn
starting while it is coming up the bore. The idea

behind starting the burn early is simple. It takes time for the mixture to burn and increase the cylinder pressure.

Sadly, time is something the engine doesn't have (at high revs there are only a few hundredths of a second for the mixture to burn), so by starting the burn early, the burn is more developed as the piston starts on its down-stroke, which is where we want maximum pressure.

It's also worth bearing in mind that as the piston travels down the bore, it increases the volume of the cylinder and reduces the pressure, weakening the effect of combustion. In fact, most of the useful work done by the burnt gas happens in the early stages of the stroke. Ignition is timed to give maximum efficiency on the power stroke.

The burn is started by the spark plug. By jumping a high voltage across a gap, a spark is produced. This excites the molecules adjacent to the spark sufficiently to start the combustion process. From there, the flame spreads out through the mixture, in much the same way as a ripple on a pond, until all the mixture is burnt or something causes it to stop.

There are several things capable of stopping the burn. Over the past few pages, we've mentioned the importance of a good even mixture several times. If the mixture is uneven, this can stop the burn. Think of it like a forest fire.

In ideal conditions, the fire will spread from tree to tree and burn the whole forest. But if the trees are too spread out (that is, they're too lean) the fire

won't be able to jump the gap and there will be areas of unburnt trees. This is what happens if there are excessively lean areas in the mixture. There are also small areas around the cylinder walls that don't burn properly because the heat energy for exciting the molecules is absorbed by the metal.

Compression ratios play a role too, and you'll normally find they are increased when an engine is tuned. By compressing the mixture, you're cramming the air and fuel molecules closer together, which makes it easy for each molecule to ignite the next. It's the same as our forest trees when they're planted very close together.

So the conditions have to be right for the mixture to burn. But if the ignition system doesn't deliver enough voltage, or there's a bad connection, the spark may not be strong enough to ignite the mixture properly or even jump the gap at all. If that happens, there will be only a partial burn or possibly no burn at all – a misfire. For this reason, it's important to keep the ignition system in good order.

It's also harder for the ignition to light a lean mixture or one under high compression. In both cases, a stronger spark is required, something that old ignitions sometimes struggled to supply. This is why there used to be lots of aftermarket ignitions for sale. It's not so much of a problem now, because bikes that need it have high-energy ignitions capable of igniting the mixture under normal conditions, and even after the engine has been tuned. They also reduce the frequency of partial burns or misfires.

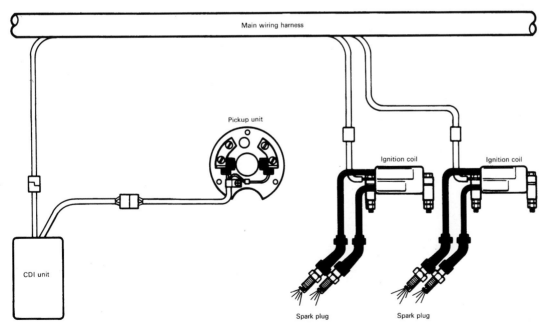

Ignition reduced to its basics

At the pickup the crank tells the CDI (a basic ECU) where it's at in its stroke. Knowing this, the CDI tells which coil to fire and when. Each pair of coils on a four-cylinder fires both its two plugs simultaneously – the so-called wasted spark, where one plug has no fresh mixture to ignite. The advantage of the system in this case is that only two coils are needed for a four-cylinder bike.

Frames

So what does your frame do? At its most basic, it keeps your backside off the floor, your wheels apart from each other, and provides a place for your engine to live. But there is much more to a frame than that.

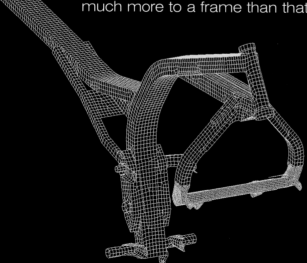

Looking beyond the fundamentals, it holds the swingarm and forks at the right heights, angles and distances to optimise handling. It must also be rigid enough to keep the wheels in line under the considerable forces of braking, acceleration and cornering. Sufficient rigidity is needed to maintain the steering head's vertical relationship to the machine and swingarm pivot's horizontal relationship regardless of the forces of turning, stopping and accelerating. The design and construction of the frame also has a role to play in insulating the rest of the machine and the rider from damaging and irritating engine vibrations.

A machine's centre of gravity is critical to how it behaves under acceleration, braking and cornering, so the frame is designed with this in mind. As you accelerate, maximum traction through the back tyre is desirable. When you brake, you want traction to be optimised at the front. When cornering, it's best if both tyres grip by the same amount and the bike turns in easily. Generally, these are all improved if the centre of gravity is high, but too high and there can be too much weight transfer, meaning wheelies and stoppies everywhere. If the centre of gravity is lower, the bike will be easier to steer, although more lean is required to make a given turn and there's less traction than with a high centre of gravity.

To provide the best of all worlds, some compromise is required in how the bike's key components are positioned.

When is an **engine** a **frame?**

Some bikes barely have a frame at all, using the engine as a so-called 'stressed member' from which the front and rear ends are hung. In these cases, the engine is effectively the frame. One of the simplest examples to illustrate the concept is the Honda 'semi-pivotless' system (as on the Blade), where the swingarm pivots round a mount at the back of the gearbox casting. Obviously that bike has a frame, as we understand them conventionally, for the front end and engine, so let's take another example of a 'proper' stressed member design. BMW's Boxers have the front as well as the rear suspension attached to the engine, with subframes carrying the rest of the bike's components.

Cradle frames

These are a very conventional design and have been around for years. The engine is bolted in a 'cradle' formed by the bottom tubes, and the head is bolted to the top rail or rails. For greater rigidity, there may be a pair of downtubes too, and larger more powerful cradle-framed bikes tend to adopt this design. The most popular material for cradle frames is steel tubing, although box-section steel is sometimes used.

Beam frames

The twin-spar, 'perimeter' or beam frame is very widely used, especially on sportsbikes. Typically two large beams join the headstock to the swingarm pivot although, as mentioned before, some bikes' swingarms pivot off the back of the gearbox. Extruded or box-section aluminium are the most common materials used in these designs, with ally castings for the swingarm pivot, although some still use steel for the whole construction. The frame wraps round the top sides of the engine to make the motor a partially stressed member, its casings being beefed up to improve load-bearing. Some beam frames also feature lower steel rails, which form an additional cradle for the engine.

Spine frames

These are popular on scooters and mopeds and are often made of pressed steel. Honda's Hornet is an example of a larger bike that uses the concept. The Hornet has a box section spine from which the engine hangs, while ally castings provide the swingarm pivot points. Spine frames are well suited to automated mass-production techniques, which explains their appeal to manufacturers of budget machines.

Trellis frames

These usually use the engine as a stressed member. Straight pieces of round or square section material, usually steel, are welded together to form lightweight but very rigid frames. The most celebrated modern example of the trellis is from Ducati. Light, minimalist, but just enough to do the job. Looks gorgeous too.

Other frame stuff

Back in the 1970s and '80s, when engine performance was rapidly eclipsing that of the chassis, a huge frame aftermarket grew up. These days, most standard frames are more than adequate. But if you fancy or require the ultra-trick, there are still plenty of companies out there that will build a bespoke frame. If you're unlucky enough to suffer a spank-up, most frames – apart from the terminally twisted – can be fixed. To check for proper true, the chassis will have to be jigged by a specialist, which means a fairly extensive stripdown. One easier way to check for damage is to look at wheel alignment (see your manual). Sometimes the damage can be seen in obvious folds and buckles in the frame. And if you're a wheelie monster, ham-fisted put-downs might lead to oval bearing housings at the headstock. Steady now.

Front suspension

The front forks are one of the busiest components on any bike. They have to optimise the tyre's contact with the road, both in a straight line and while cornering. They must smooth the ride over uneven surfaces and minimise dive under braking. Then they also need to give the rider adequate feedback about what the front end's doing in any circumstance. Quite a lot to be going on with.

As far as the basic anatomy of motorcycle forks goes, stanchions (also known as sliders) travel up and down the fork leg. There are two basic types in common use these days – right way up (RWU), stanchion above leg and upside down (USD), stanchion below leg. There are other systems, but telescopic forks are by far the most common.

Rebound damping *While the springs will bounce back merrily on their own, the rebound damping uses oil/or sometimes gas forced through valves to slow the process.*

Preload *adjuster takes up sag in the front springs. Doesn't make the spring 'harder', although it can feel that way.*

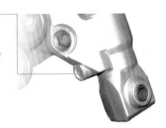

Compression damping *as with the rebound, uses oil and sometimes gas to slow the bike's progress down the fork's travel.*

Springs

Internal springs take care of the basic rates of dive and rebound. At their cheapest and most basic, springs have equally wound coils, which compress evenly. Because this simple type doesn't become stiffer as it compresses, there's a risk of the forks bottoming out when severe bumps are encountered at speed. Better than these are multi-rate springs, which can be two springs of different strengths, or single springs wound to different rates at either end. The softer spring takes care of smaller bumps and shocks, and as it compresses completely, the second stronger spring or section of spring takes effect.

Best of all are 'progressive' springs, where the distance between the spring's coils gets progressively less along the length of the spring. Progressive springs become stiffer as they compress and less stiff as they lengthen, the rate of which is optimised to account for the weight of the bike and that of a typical rider. The progressive nature of the springs means that small bumps are easily absorbed, and sudden larger bumps can be dealt with without the forks bottoming out.

Damping

When you hit a bump, the fork springs compress. The next thing they want to do is to extend, pushing the bike up – the energy they've just absorbed has to go somewhere. A series of bumps has the potential to tie suspension in knots, the bike bumping and jarring over the irregular surface.

Damping is the method of governing the rate at which the forks dive (compress) and spring back (rebound). Some mopeds, scooters and lightweights get by with no damping at all or rely on friction.

Oil damping is used on other machines. Valves control the rate at which the oil passes on compression and rebound. Gas and air have also been used to assist the damping.

Front suspension adjustment

Budget and smaller capacity bikes often have non-adjustable suspension, and for most riders of these machines, the absence of adjusters will go unnoticed. On larger bikes, particularly sportsbikes and tourers, there are usually four main adjustable factors – preload, height of forks in the yokes, rebound damping and compression damping.

Preload adjustment is found at the top of the forks and alters the effective length of the springs. It doesn't make the suspension softer or harder, but varies the ride height and the amount the bike 'sags' on its suspension. Rebound adjusters are usually concentric with and internal to the preload adjusters and dictate the rate the forks extend after compression. At the bottom of the forks are the compression adjusters, which can be tweaked to control the rate of dive.

When your bike left the dealership when it was new, the suspension should have been set to the base setting suggested by the manufacturer in the owner's manual. These are invariably a best average, for average road conditions, riding style and rider weight. But no road or rider conforms to an average, so feel free to fiddle with the adjusters. Just remember to do it gradually.

And unless you've bought the latest homologation race replica sportsbike, your bike's suspension has been built down to a price. That's not to say it won't meet your needs – and lots of standard forks are excellent – but if you're a trackday demon or an ace on the roads, you might want something with more adjustment. Look at revalving the standard kit or replacing the springs. Or if you want to go all the way, buy some trick aftermarket forks.

Rear
suspension

Like the front forks, the rear shock (or shocks on a twin-shock bike) has plenty to do to. It has to optimise tyre contact with the road in a straight line and in corners; smooth the ride over uneven surfaces; and give the rider feedback about what the tyre's up to. Yet the rear suspension also has an important role in ensuring as much power as possible is delivered to the road without wheelspin or excessive compression and extension. If your bike had no rear suspension and any appreciable power, the back wheel would spend as much time off the road as it would in contact with it.

What's in a shock?

An external spring takes care of the basic rates of dive and rebound and, like the springs in the front forks, it is often 'progressive' or 'multi-rate', so it becomes stiffer as it compresses. As with the front suspension, progressive springs provide a more effective solution than multi-rate springs, which are just two springs of different rates.

On many monoshock bikes, a rising-rate linkage, connecting the shock to the swingarm and frame, means a cheaper-to-manufacture constant-rate spring can be used. All these methods prevent the travel being used up too quickly by severe bumps while making the spring compliant enough to deal with more moderate bumps.

That spring lives outside a damper unit, which is typically oil-filled to control the rates of shock compression and rebound. The oil passes through shim stacks (a bit like washers), which restrict the rate it can pass at.

Shock adjustment

Cheap shocks, as found on budget bikes and many smaller machines, tend to rely on stiff springs and basic damping. More sophisticated shocks combine better multi-rate springs with adjustable damping for improved performance. Many use compressed gas to keep the oil under pressure, which prevents bubbles forming in it and damping being lost when the shock is working hard and fast. Apart from compression and rebound adjusters, some high-end shocks have additional high-speed damping adjusters to give the rear additional help when particularly violent bumps are encountered. Some have ride height adjusters

too to raise the back of the bike and quicken steering.

Rear shock preload adjustment is usually by stepped collar or threaded rings on the shock body. Increasing it reduces sag and the bike sits a little higher. Remote preload adjusters are fitted to some shocks for ease of adjustment. Rebound adjustment is generally found at the bottom of the shock and compression at the top, sometimes on a remote adjuster.

Some shocks are non-adjustable, but it is often possible to fit springs of different rates and have the shock revalved or filled with a different grade of oil to change the way the unit behaves. There are plenty of specialists offering these services.

Most shocks on mass-produced bikes are built down to a budget, but as with front forks, many are excellent and more than adequate for all but racers and trackday nuts. Revalving and springs of different rates are the cheapest ways to tailor the standard equipment to your needs. There's a huge aftermarket out there for riders who simply want replacements and those that want extra performance, providing shocks that are often better and cheaper than original equipment.

The location of monoshocks in particular on a bike means they can get covered in road dirt and water flung off the back wheel. Fitting a hugger will protect the shock from the worst of this. They can run very hot as well because, apart from heat generated in the unit through its operation, it's also sited close to the engine and is away from the flow of cooling air. For that reason, damping systems have become progressively better over the years, especially in high-end shocks. Some keep the damping medium in a separate reservoir sited either remotely or on the back of the shock.

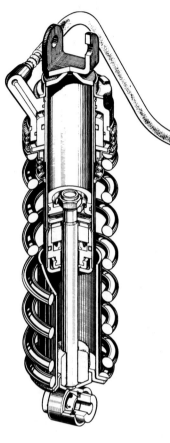

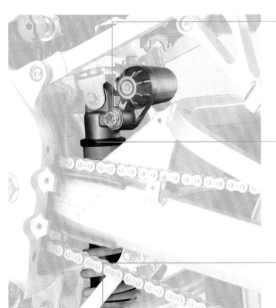

Compression damping Like on the front end oil damping slows the rate of dive. Gas is almost always involved on bigger bikes to help the oil hydraulics out.

Preload This particular shock lacks a remote preload adjuster, making C-spanner induced skinned knuckles a near certainty.

Rebound damping This shock has a screw adjuster for rebound damping which slows the rate the shock extends at. Some others use knurled knobs.

Swingarms

Most swingarms supplied as standard on modern bikes are up to the job they're designed to do. Fundamentally they carry the back wheel, pivot off the back of the frame or engine, and are prevented from slamming the tyre into the underside of the seat by the shocks or monoshock and its linkage.

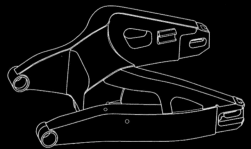

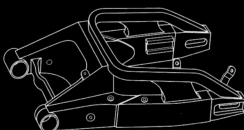

Huge as they are, these ally swingarms provide several times the rigidity of steel for proportionately less weight and allow plenty of bracing to be used for little mass trade-off.

There's a lot more going on beyond the basic functions of a swingarm. As with frames, rigidity is an issue. In the old days, tubular swingarms on puny mounts allowed the wheel to flex sideways, which upset handling, but at that time the power of the bikes and their tyres were such that there weren't too many demands on the (just about) adequate chassis of the era. Gusseting between the two forks of the swingarm and the pivot tube helped prevent flex. The usual material was tubular steel, but as power outputs rose and bikes got better, manufacturers started to use box section designs. The only problem was that the weight penalty started to increase as the section of these swingarms got bigger in line with further power hikes. Bracing got bigger and heavier too.

Modern swing

Today, things are different. Many bikes still use steel swingarms, but tubular ones are usually found only on twin-shock lightweights. Steel box section swingarms are still quite common too, particularly on middleweight budget roadsters.

Aluminium is the thing these days, particularly on high-performance bikes. Obviously it's lighter than steel but not as strong, although an alloy swingarm that's as strong and heavy as a steel arm is stiffer. So it's possible to build alloy swingarms that are just as stiff as steel but lighter. Ally items are often internally and externally braced for more strength. This means the walls of the swingarm can be thinner and hence lighter.

Taking sides

Single-sided swingarms are a race-bred option designed for easy wheel changes in endurance competition. Hyper-rigid, but there's a weight penalty. Ducati top-end sportsbikes have them (although the race bikes use magnesium or carbon while the less exotic street machines use alloy), but the Triumph 955i has gone back to a more conventional system. Until recently Ducatis used a single-sider pivoting on the crankcase rather than the back of the gearbox or frame, as would be usual practice, because of their long V-twin engines, which had to be mounted far back in the frame because of the cylinder sticking out the front. The Duke's wheelbase would have been too great for quick steering if it used a conventionally mounted swingarm that was long enough to accommodate wheel and shock.

Weight watchers

Swingarms play a big part in the knotty problem of unsprung weight – that's to say, those components which live below your bike's suspension, such as wheels, brakes and swingarms. An amount of the suspension system's weight adds to the unsprung load too. Basically, the lower the proportion of unsprung weight to the sprung mass of the bike (the rest of it), the better the handling. The main reason for this is because unsprung mass gathers momentum on the move, upsetting the suspension. Therefore, a heavy bike on lighter running gear tends to be more composed than a pared-down sportster on the same chassis.

Swing out

So swingarms are a compromise between rigidity and weight. Many aftermarket options offer extra rigidity but not much of a weight advantage. A full works racing swingarm made from something exotic like magnesium or carbon fibre would offer the best of all worlds, but unless you're a full works rider, you probably won't feel any advantage.

There is a healthy swingarm aftermarket too, which first emerged in the old days of flexi-frames and swingarms. Often beautifully engineered with trick bracing, they can also offer the option of adjusting the wheelbase and revised shock linkages. Even these days, the bike manufacturers don't always get it exactly right, so there will always be room for aftermarket specialists.

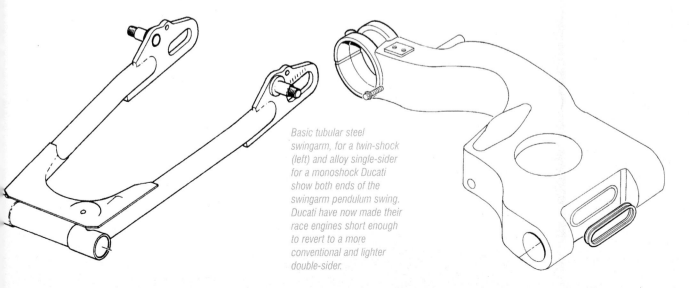

Basic tubular steel swingarm, for a twin-shock (left) and alloy single-sider for a monoshock Ducati show both ends of the swingarm pendulum swing. Ducati have now made their race engines short enough to revert to a more conventional and lighter double-sider.

Wheels

Wheels take quite a pounding from the forces of acceleration, braking, the weight of the motorcycle, and irregular road surfaces and potholes. Wheels fall into two main categories – wire-spoked and cast.

A wire-spoked wheel (left) usually looks flimsy next to a cast sportsbike item. The Oz item on this Aprilia (right) is the exception that proves the rule. Light weight with strength.

Wire wheels

Wire-spoked wheels are less common these days but still find a place on some lightweight road bikes, customs, retros and off-road machines. This last type of bike uses them because of their light weight and ability to take the punishment handed out by off-road riding, thanks in part to their inherent flexibility. BMW's GS series is one exception to the general road bike rule, although it must be said that the GS claims some off-road capability too. The BMW has spoked wheels cleverly laced to allow the use of tubeless tyres – the spokes sit outboard of the tyre bead. Moto Guzzi has adopted a similar system. Tubeless tyres cannot be used on conventional spoked wheels because the air would leak out of the spoke holes.

Cast wheels

Cast wheels have become the norm for most bikes because they're light enough, strong and easy to mass-produce. It wouldn't take long for a modern high-powered superbike to break all the spokes in a wire wheel. In any case, modern radial tyre designs are tubeless, so cast wheels are the obvious choice for most applications. Cast wheels are usually made from a one-piece casting incorporating hub, rim and spokes, unlike the three separate elements of a wire-spoked wheel.

Like so many refinements on modern bikes, cast wheels came from the racing scene, where they were originally made from exotic alloys to cut down on weight. Another advantage was that the hubs could be made narrower than on spoked wheels, allowing more room for the fitment of disc brakes.

The cast wheels on mass-produced road-going machines are made of ordinary aluminium alloys, which are just as stiff but more robust and cheaper (if heavier) than magnesium. However, some top-end production sportsbikes are now being graced with mag wheels and they are available as an aftermarket option.

The wheel deal

The most important thing for a wheel is that it's round. That's not being flippant. If a wheel runs out of true, perhaps because it's been damaged, handling can be upset, tyres wear unevenly and tubeless tyres can deflate. Some run-out is permissible, but if in doubt, have it checked out. Wire-spoked wheels can be trued up if the run-out isn't too bad, and it is possible to have cast wheels repaired, provided the structural integrity of the wheel isn't compromised. But any chunks out of the rim, cracked cast spokes or folds in the rim mean it must be replaced. Also, cast wheels can suffer fractures invisible to the naked eye in an impact, so if you have any doubts, have the wheels checked out by an engineering specialist.

It's important that you have the right tyres on your wheels, that they are correctly aligned and that the bearings are good. See the 'Tyres' and 'Looking after your bike' sections for more information on these areas.

Lighten up

There's a big aftermarket wheel industry, ranging from builders of spoked wheels to companies making competition wheels out of exotic materials such as carbon fibre and magnesium and other light alloys. Apart from looking seriously trick, some of the latter can offer significant savings in unsprung weight. For a basic explanation of this, see the previous pages on swingarms. Another advantage is that light front wheels can help steering because there's less gyroscopic effect to overcome. To understand gyroscopic effect, next time you've got a wheel out of a pushbike, hold the axle and get a friend to set it spinning. Now move your hands up and down and side to side. You'll feel some strong forces at play. But as with most things in biking, there's a compromise. Heavier wheels help with straight-line stability, which is why Honda specifies a heavy tyre for the Gold Wing.

Brakes

Unless you happen to be a speedway rider, you'll appreciate the importance of decent brakes. Apart from a few lightweights, scooters, retros and customs, it tends to be disc brakes all round these days – and even many of the bikes that feature drums on the back opt for discs up front.

Drum brakes

We'll keep it brief on the less common drum brakes. These work by forcing friction-material-lined shoes into contact with the steel or iron-lined inside of the drum by way of a cable or rod-operated cam or cams. Return springs pull the shoes clear of the drum when the brake levers are released.

They do their job adequately on low-powered, light bikes – provided the drum is true, the steel liner is not too worn, the shoes have got enough material on them and the cable's in good nick.

Drum brakes are less efficient at dispersing heat than disc systems. Before the widespread use of disc set-ups, huge drums were used on race bikes and larger road bikes. Under hard use, these brakes would start to 'fade' as the heat built up and braking efficiency was lost.

Drum brakes Simple in operation, but not up to the power, speed and low maintenance requirements of most of today's bikes and riders.

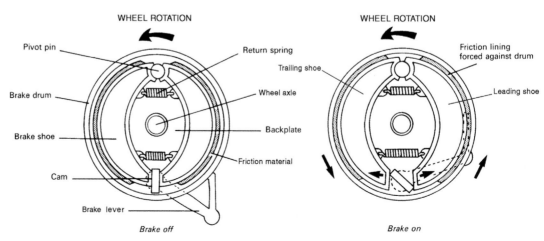

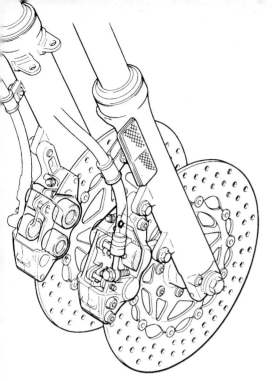

Disc brakes

Disc brakes are far more efficient than drums. We have the aviation industry to thank for disc brakes, but it took a few decades for them to evolve into the hyper-powerful systems used on bikes today.

Pistons operated hydraulically in the calipers from the front or rear master cylinders act on the steel backs of the friction pads, which squeeze the disc.

It's important that the calipers are designed to be rigid. If they were able to flex as the brakes were applied, their efficiency would diminish.

The most basic caliper has a single piston pushing one pad and slides to pull the other (fixed) pad against the disc. An opposed piston caliper has a pair or pairs of pistons pushing the pads. Multi-piston calipers are common on the front of bikes. Four piston (also more commonly known as four-pot) calipers are widely used. Kawasaki, for example, fits Tokico six-pots to some of its sportsbikes. Certain aftermarket calipers have more still. But it's not just down to the number of pistons. Their area and their relationship (ratio) with the master cylinder at the lever is important too; likewise the area of the pads. The piston at the master cylinder has a small area, where the area of the piston(s) in the caliper is large. This gives rise to something called the 'hydraulic multiplier effect', which means that relatively little force at the lever results in far greater forces at the caliper. Different-sized pistons are being used in certain individual calipers now-adays to provide more progressive braking. When you stop applying the brakes, the disc 'pushes' the pad away slightly and a rubber seal between the caliper and piston, shaped to twist a little as the piston moves out, pulls it back in again.

Multi-pot calipers allow longer, narrower pads to be used, meaning the area of the disc they operate on can be narrower and therefore lighter, reducing unsprung weight and gyroscopic forces (see 'Swingarms' and 'Wheels' for explanations of these).

Discs and pads

Discs are usually steel or iron. There's a limit to how narrow and thin they can be, because they have to be strong and there's a lot of heat to dissipate. On many modern designs, the disc can 'float' slightly on its carrier to optimise pad contact and allow a little room for heat expansion, preventing warpage.

Pad friction material is most commonly sintered metal these days because it works well in the wet – something early disc systems tended not to do. Different compounds are available for different applications. Hard brakers and trackday riders will have different requirements from touring riders, for example.

High-end race bikes feature carbon brakes (pads and discs), but the amount of heat that has to be in them to make them work means that they're no good for road bikes.

Likewise, full-on race compound pads might not work as well for standard brake set-ups on the road as they do on the track, although there are many aftermarket pads that offer performance superior to standard kit for everyday use.

Other braking points

Some bikes feature linked braking systems, where application of either the front or rear brake will lead to complete or partial application of the other brake. This is not to every rider's taste, many preferring individual control of the brakes, although the manufacturers do design these systems for balanced braking.

Other machines feature anti-lock braking systems, usually available as an optional extra, which allow riders to brake as hard as they like without skidding.

The efficiency of your disc brakes relies on correct maintenance of the brake system and periodic changes of the correct type of brake fluid. See your manual or the 'Looking after your bike' section of this book for more details.

Disc brakes *Schematic of typical production system on left. Note small diameter yet high bulk of discs. PFM aftermarket system on right has skinny braking area of greater diameter, allowing light but long calipers making for high swept area yet low unsprung weight.*

Radial brakes *Another feature inherited from the world of racing, radially mounted calipers flex less than conventional types. This extra efficiency means that smaller calipers and discs can be used, reducing unsprung weight and gyroscopic forces making for quicker, easier steering. Petal discs dissipate heat produced by braking more efficiently.*

Chassis accessories

There are aftermarket options for every chassis part we've discussed in this chapter, but there are other useful items you might want to consider too.

Grab rails Many bikes, especially sportsbikes, are less than generous in pillion provision. There are aftermarket grab rails to give a passenger something to grab hold of if they don't want to get too intimate with the rider in the absence of standard-fit grab rails.

Huggers Most monoshock bikes have very little protection from road dirt and the elements for the rear shock and its linkages. A hugger mounted to the swingarm will reduce the amount of water and muck being thrown at the shock, swingarm and back of the engine. Most replace the standard chainguard too. There's no problem of fit with better ones, but make sure cheaper items offer enough clearance for the tyre and chain. An undertray for the rear seat unit makes that area easy to clean and keeps crud out.

Rearsets Hard road riders and trackday fanatics might find that standard footpegs don't offer enough ground clearance. Aftermarket rearsets mount the pegs and controls higher and further back to help with this. Many have a huge range of adjustment for peg position to let riders set them for maximum comfort.

Crash bungs *Motorcycle bodywork and cycle parts are expensive, so it's worth considering a set of crash bungs just in case the worst happens. Don't go for the cheap minimalist ones that will quickly disappear at the first hint of impact. Buy the type that bolt properly through frame and engine mount. This might mean some drilling of the fairing lowers, but it's worth it if they do their job and prevent your fairing and frame being written off.*

Clip-ons *If you've gone for racy rearsets, you might find that the handlebars are now in the wrong place. Aftermarket clip-ons usually offer more adjustment than the standard bars fitted to your bike and there's often a weight benefit. Going the* other way, riders who find the riding position of their bike too extreme might like to consider bar risers. Remember that cables and hoses might now be too long or too short. Check that everything can still operate freely.

Screens *For bikes without screens, there are plenty of bolt-on options to offer a little weather protection. If you have a faired bike and find the standard screen inadequate, there are higher and double-bubble alternatives. But be aware that sometimes all these do is move the windblast to an equally uncomfortable part of your anatomy.*

Steering dampers *These hydraulic units are designed to prevent tank-slappers (where the bars wobble uncontrollably from side to side) and improve stability. Usually adjustable for damping, they connect between the frame and the forks. The chassis geometry of most modern bikes makes them sufficiently stable most of the time. But some bikes with more radical geometry for quick steering, particularly sportsbikes, can suffer from shakes and wobbles when pushed hard. A decent damper reduces the problem. Some high-end sportsbikes have them as standard, but there's a ready aftermarket supply for bikes that don't, or as improvements over the original equipment.*

Braided brake hoses *These are now fitted as standard on some bikes, but if not they make a huge difference in feel to disc brake set-ups, being less prone to expansion than conventional pipes. Stainless and Kevlar are popular materials for the braided outers of the hoses. The banjos that join the hose to the caliper are available in plated or stainless steel and alloy, but alloy should really only be used on race bikes since road salt can cause dangerous corrosion.*

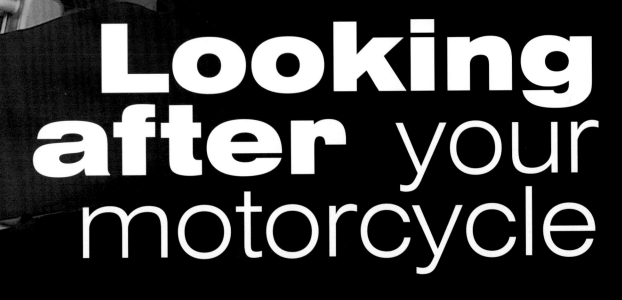

Looking after your motorcycle

4

Tools &
maintenance

Maintenance is vitally important. Just a few simple checks – even a quick glance before you ride – often makes the difference between catching a problem early, and expensive repairs later. It can even help to prevent an accident.

On any vehicle, things wear out, break and come loose. After all, it's simply a collection of parts asked to do fairly extreme things. Just think about the forces acting on a bike and you can imagine how important it is to check that spindles are tight and there's oil in the engine. Of course, you're not going to prevent all failures with maintenance. The idea is simply to prevent the obvious ones so you can spend more time enjoying riding your bike and less time getting it fixed at the dealer.

A comprehensive list of daily and weekly checks can be found in the user's manual, but if you haven't got one, the list of what to check is pretty simple. Once a week, you should check tyre

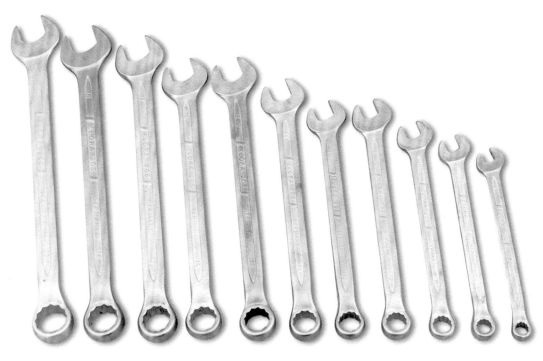

This is a reasonably comprehensive set of combination (open one end, ring the other) spanners for bike work. Double up on the more popular sizes.

pressures, oil levels and cable adjustments. You should know whether most of these things need adjusting as you ride.

Also, before you ride, just glance at the nuts and bolts you can see. Are any sticking out, indicating they're loose? It does happen, even on brand new machines. If the engine takes longer and longer to start each time you ride, it's a sign that something is beginning to fail, even if it's just the battery. But catching it early means you won't be left stranded. So even with a little mechanical knowledge, you can save yourself money and have peace of mind that certain jobs have been done.

You'll find explanations and suggestions of what to check in the next few sections. By breaking the bike down into sections, looking after it seems less daunting. And as you become more familiar with working on bikes, you should be able to tackle more complicated jobs with ease. The first things you'll need are tools and it's worth making sure you have the right ones.

Tools are an essential part of looking after your bike. Good quality tools of the correct type will enable you to deal with jobs properly. You don't need roll-cabs and chests reaching to the shed roof, but a few quality essentials will go a long way.

Spanners

First and foremost are spanners. A set ranging from 7 to 19mm is good enough to tackle the majority of the fasteners on most modern bikes, although you may want to get two 10, 12 and 13mm spanners since they're popular sizes and sometimes it takes two to undo a component. Owners of some older British and American classics will need the appropriate imperial sizes for their machine. Buy combination spanners – they have an open end and a ring end. There are numerous jaw and ring designs and the more expensive spanners drive on the flats of the fasteners rather than the corners. But don't worry too much about this: quality and comfort are the priorities. Buy the best you can afford, and if you find over time that the most commonly used spanners in the set are wearing badly, replace these with higher quality items. Car boot sales are a great source of second-hand tools for people on a budget, and your money might be better spent there rather than on cheap and nasty new stuff. A couple of small adjustable spanners are a worthy addition to your toolkit, but they're not as good as non-adjustable types because they are often more prone to slipping on fasteners, rounding them off.

This ring spanner drives on the flats of nut and bolt heads, reducing the risk of rounding off through better contact with the component.

This spanner offers more angles of attack, but drives on the corners, giving nuts and bolts a harder time.

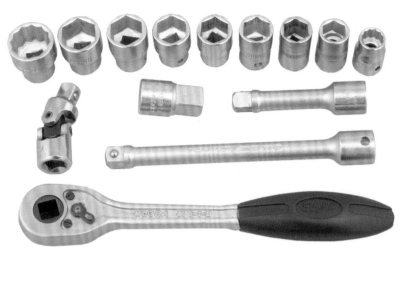

Socket sets

A socket set is vital. As with spanners, cheap stuff is a no-no, so the set you got free with a tenner's worth of petrol will not do the job. Quality is inferior and they're usually useless sizes anyway.

For bike work, $1/4$, $3/8$ and $1/2$in are the most popular drive sizes, with sockets ranging from 6mm to 24mm in the best sets. Owners of old classics will again require imperial sets. Most sockets have a 12-point design, allowing the socket to fit in more positions and grip bolt heads and nuts snugly, avoiding rounding. However, a six-point design is better in some ways since it's more tolerant of fasteners that have already been slightly rounded. Once you've removed any such fasteners, it's a good idea to replace them with new ones – you might not be so lucky in removing them next time.

Allen, Torx and spline bits are available to fit socket drives, as well as oil filter spinners. Torx and spline-headed bolts are also used occasionally, and you'll need the appropriate sockets.

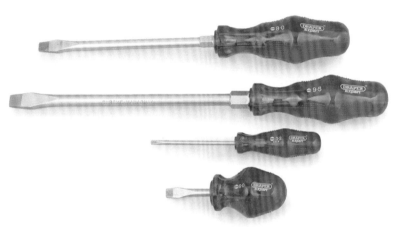

Screwdrivers

It's worth buying good quality screwdrivers as the heads of screws are normally the first casualties of home servicing. Buy screwdrivers with good tips and comfortable handles. A selection of Phillips and flat-bladed screwdrivers is enough for most jobs. Be sure to use the screwdriver that has the best fit to the screw slots you're attacking. If you intend to strip engines, an impact driver that can take sockets as well as screwdriver bits is handy.

Allen keys

Most modern bikes use Allen bolts to hold various things together, so a good set of keys is essential. Better than the classic key shape, consider getting a set of T-bars and some socket-Allen keys. You can use the socket keys to loosen tight bolts and the T-bars to remove them quickly. The most common sizes are 4–8mm, although try to go a little either side of this. Torx and spline keys will be required for some other fasteners.

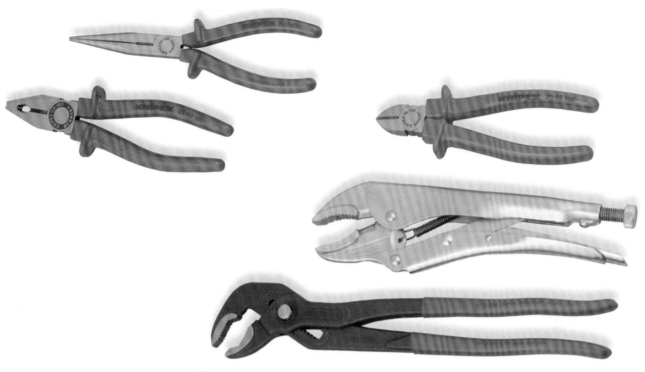

Pliers

As well as a standard set of pliers, long-handled snipe-nose pliers are extremely useful for working on bikes. They allow you to reach deep into the bike through limited gaps. A set of vice-grip pliers will also make life easier.

Torque wrenches

For reassembly, a torque wrench is essential to ensure fasteners are tightened to the correct figures as given in your workshop manual. This will avoid snapped fasteners, stripped threads and distorted casings, or worse. There are two types: the beam type, which uses a pointer on a calibrated scale to show the applied torque; and the pre-set type, where the torque is set with an adjuster and the tool 'gives' or clicks when the fastener is at the proper tightness. You'll need a torque wrench suited towards bike work (the majority of settings needed for bikes are lower than for cars). A tool with a range of 7–100Nm should suffice.

Tool care

Look after your tools and they'll give you years of service. A squirt of WD40 and a wipe with a rag after use is wise. Store them in a decent toolbox, kept in a dry place. If you try to apply some logic to which tool goes where in the box, you'll also save yourself hours of frustration hunting for the right tool.

Cleaning

Cleaning bikes is important. Apart from keeping your bike looking tidy and new for longer, which increases the amount of money you'll get when you resell it, this is a good way of spotting problems before they become too major.

A range of specialist bike-cleaning potions and implements. Beats a sponge and a bucket full of warm water and washing-up liquid. Although that's better than nothing.

When race bikes are cleaned, the mechanics aren't just trying to keep the sponsors happy. As they clean the wheels, they'll be looking for cracks or dents. It's the same with the frame and other parts. Cleaning is the best way of spotting problems before they get serious.

The first thing to do is get rid of the thicker gunge, which, at the rear, normally comes in the form of old chain lube. Some paraffin or other degreaser on a rag will cut through this, and it must be rinsed away afterwards. Avoid using petrol as a degreaser. Apart from being highly flammable, you don't want to get it on your skin. It can also attack some plastic and rubber parts on bikes. Applying degreaser by rag reduces the chances of it getting where it shouldn't, such as in the wheel bearings.

Fresh brake dust can normally be wiped off wheels easily. But old dust, and dust on the calipers, normally needs agitating, which is best done with a short-bristled paint brush or old toothbrush. You can also get special brake dust removing sprays, which are pretty good. Some specialist wheel cleaning fluids are slightly corrosive. Make sure you don't spray or brush any on to unlaquered aluminium. Remember to clean dust from inside the caliper too, and use only brake cleaner or fresh brake fluid. Other solvents might attack the hydraulic seals.

The rest of the bike can be washed normally with water and detergent (dedicated detergent is better than washing-up liquid) then polished. There's a bewildering array of specialised cleaning products on the market. But for general cleaning, you can do all these jobs with one product. Domestic general polishes like Mr Sheen are often ideal. They remove chain lube, dried-on flies, brake dust and clean and polish at the same time – so you only have to do the job once. For dried-on flies and chain lube, spray it on liberally and leave for a minute or two. But try not to do it in conditions where the spray will dry. And remember to use a clean rag on your screen and paintwork. Whole screens have needed replacing because the rag used on them was the same one that cleaned a gritty area of bodywork.

If you're serious about cleaning, or your bike gets particularly filthy, you might want to invest in a jet washer. But don't be too vigourous around wheel, head, swingarm and shock bearings and linkages, since the grease can be forced out, which accelerates wear. The same goes for the chain, so be sure to lubricate it after jet washing.

With your bike cleaned, application of a good polish will bring out the shine, and silicon types claim to provide longer resistance to dirt build-up. Don't go too mad too often with paint-restoring polishes as these are usually mildly abrasive and you might wind up going through the paint. Use specialist polishes on bare aluminium and chrome, a favourite pastime of retro, cruiser and classic enthusiasts.

Chain care

Chains do a lot of work in harsh conditions, so periodic maintenance is essential. Ideally, chains should be inspected every 600 miles. Even a quick once-over and some lube is better than nothing and will increase chain life considerably. The three important chain care jobs are cleaning, adjustment and lubrication.

It's important to keep chains clean because grit and other dirt sticks to the lube and acts as a grinding paste, speeding up the wear process. Clean the chain with something like paraffin to cut through built up lube and then give it a good rinse. Don't leave the paraffin on the chain for ages, though.

Once clean, let the chain dry. If you spray on lube when it's still wet, you'll be trapping in moisture. It's important to know what type of chain you have fitted. Most bikes have O-ring chains, with rubber rings holding lubricant inside the rollers. These should be lubricated with O-ring chain lube. In this case, the lube will protect the outside of the chain and keep the O-rings supple and the grease inside the chain, rather than lubricating the pins.

No matter what type of chain, lube is best applied after a ride, when the chain is warm. This allows better penetration of the lube. When lubing chains,

direct it so it hits in between the plates on both sides of the chain. Also, if you apply it to the lower run of the chain, centrifugal force will take care of lubing the outside. After a few minutes, wipe away any excess – it'll only fling off and make more mess elsewhere.

Automatic oilers are worth a mention because they save time and effort once fitted and extend chain life considerably. They also increase the time required between chain adjustments.

When adjusting chains, it's not only chain tension that's important. Wheel alignment is as crucial and should be checked carefully. Nearly all chain adjusters have some form of indicator, but if you have the time, it's worth double-checking wheel alignment using straight edges or a length of string because some adjusters can be out.

Checking chain tension and wear

To find out the correct tension and permissible chain stretch, check your manual.

With your bike upright (but not with someone sitting on it) and in neutral, push the bottom chain run down and measure the slack midway between the two sprockets. Rotate the rear wheel slightly and check again. Do this at several points along the chain because they wear unevenly, which leads to tight spots. Adjust for the correct tension at the tightest point on the chain.

If your chain is at, or close to, the end of its adjustment, it's worn out. This is best checked with the chain off the bike but can be done while it is still fitted. To do this, remove the chainguard and, with the chain taut, measure a number of links along the top run. Then see how the measurements compare to the spec in your manual. Rotate the rear wheel

and measure various sections of the chain in this way. Any kinking, frozen links or missing O-rings mean that it's time for a new chain.

Check front and rear sprockets for signs of wear too. If either sprocket has teeth that appear bent or 'hooked', do not be tempted to reverse the sprocket – this could lead to sudden failure because the teeth could break off. If either chain or sprockets are worn, replace as a set since one worn item will hasten the wear of the others.

Adjustment

Assuming that the chain and sprockets are still good, they can be adjusted. With the tightest point of the chain at the centre of the bottom run and the bike supported upright (again without someone sitting on it, so either prop the bike securely or have someone hold it from the front), first slacken the wheel spindle. Now loosen the locknuts for the sliding adjusters' screws and turn them equally until the chain is at the correct tension as specified in your manual. Check the wheel alignment marks are in the same place on each side, and that everything is butting up as it should. If not, push the wheel forward or pull it back until they are. Check alignment marks and chain tension again. Once satisfied with everything, tighten the spindle to the correct torque setting in your manual and tighten the locknuts. Make a final check of the chain tension before riding.

Things are slightly different on bikes with eccentric adjusters and single-sided swingarms, but correct chain tension is equally important. Refer to your manual for detailed advice on adjustment.

Remember that if a chain is too tight, it can cause havoc with gearboxes and bearings.

Direct chain lube so it gets between the plates on both sides of the chain. It's best to direct the spray at the lower run while the chain's warm, i.e. after a ride.

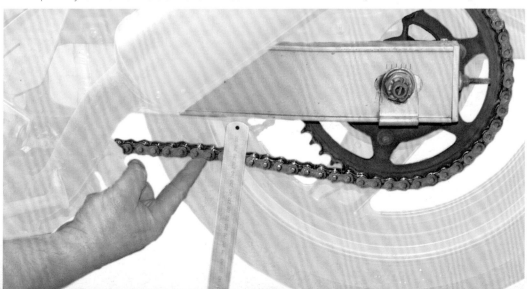

Look for the tightest point on the chain, then adjust as per the measurements in your manual. Some do it by feel. If in doubt use a ruler as shown here.

Brakes

The most important thing about any machine is its capacity to stop. That's why it's vital to keep brakes in good condition, so it stops when you ask it to. All bikes, no matter what their intended use, will use disc or drum brake systems or a combination of both.

Master cylinder reservoir
Check fluid level often, and if it decreases quickly check for leaks in the system. Murky fluid is contaminated and the system should be bled to replace it.

Brake hoses
Most bikes have lines with rubber-type outers that allow expansion over time leading to spongy brakes. Braided hoses are better.

Brake discs
Must be outside minimum thickness. They must also be unwarped or the brakes will judder.

Calipers
Tend to attract road dirt impeding efficiency. Keep 'em clean with regular applications of brake cleaner. Check often for pad wear.

Inspection

The most important thing to check on disc or drum brake systems is the amount of friction material left on the pads or shoes (drum brakes have shoes, discs have pads). The material wears every time the brakes are applied and often wears faster than you might think.

You can check pads simply by looking through the caliper because many pads have wear indicators visible without the need to remove the calipers, but on multi-disc systems bear in mind that pads don't wear evenly. Check all the pads and never allow them to wear so far that the backing plate damages the discs. Drum brakes are harder to inspect and can sometimes require wheel removal, although most drums have wear indicators, which make life easier.

Replacing disc brake pads

Replacing brake pads means removing the calipers and pushing the pistons back with a piece of wood to accommodate the new pads. But before you do this, be sure to clean the pistons as best you can. If you simply push them back, dirt and brake dust can be forced back into the caliper, which can stop the pistons withdrawing properly when you let go of the lever. A squirt of brake cleaner and a wipe is normally adequate.

But be aware that the fluid level can rise as the pistons go back and some may have to be siphoned off. Be careful not to get fluid on paintwork or plastics – it can attack them in seconds.

If necessary, add more brake fluid of the correct type as you pump the calipers up after refitting. Do not allow air to enter the system by letting the fluid level get too low, and make sure you have pumped the brake lever to put the pads back in contact with the disc before riding.

Other brake maintenance

Apart from the pads wearing, there is little else that requires attention. Hydraulic disc systems are self-adjusting, and the only thing to watch is the fluid level in the reservoir. The fluid should be renewed as per the service intervals suggested in your manual.

As the pads wear, more fluid will be taken into the system to take up the slack. If the level drops below the minimum, there is again a chance air will be drawn into the system, which reduces its effectiveness dramatically, making the controls feel spongy. Take a regular look at fluid level indicators on the master cylinders and never let the level drop below the minimum mark. If air does enter the system, the brakes will have to be bled properly.

As drum brake shoes wear, slack in the cables and brake rods will have to be taken up. Check the bike's manual for details of your system. Cables must be in good condition and must be kept correctly adjusted and lubricated.

Disc and drum surfaces need checking too. Discs should be inspected for cracks, as should drums. Discs and drums should also be measured for wear and distortion, and replaced if necessary. The minimum thicknesses are normally stamped on the parts, and can also be found in your manual.

On disc brake systems, the brake fluid, hydraulic seals and hoses degrade over time and must be renewed in accordance with your bike's service schedule. Inspect hoses and unions regularly for signs of leaks and corrosion at the banjos. Brake fluid is hygroscopic and absorbs moisture from the atmosphere over time, impairing braking efficiency and giving a spongy feel at the lever or pedal. So don't neglect replacing it with the correct fluid at the specified intervals, and certainly no more than every couple of years, regardless of mileage. Always use new fluid from a sealed container.

Do not work on a bike's braking system unless you're confident you know what you're doing. Your Haynes manual shows you the correct procedures; for safety's sake follow them to the letter.

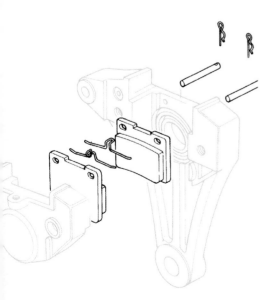

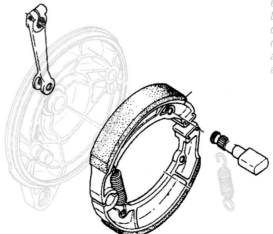

Basic disc caliper (left) and even more basic drum. Don't worry about what type of brakes your bike has too much, they're usually adequate. Pay more attention to maintenance.

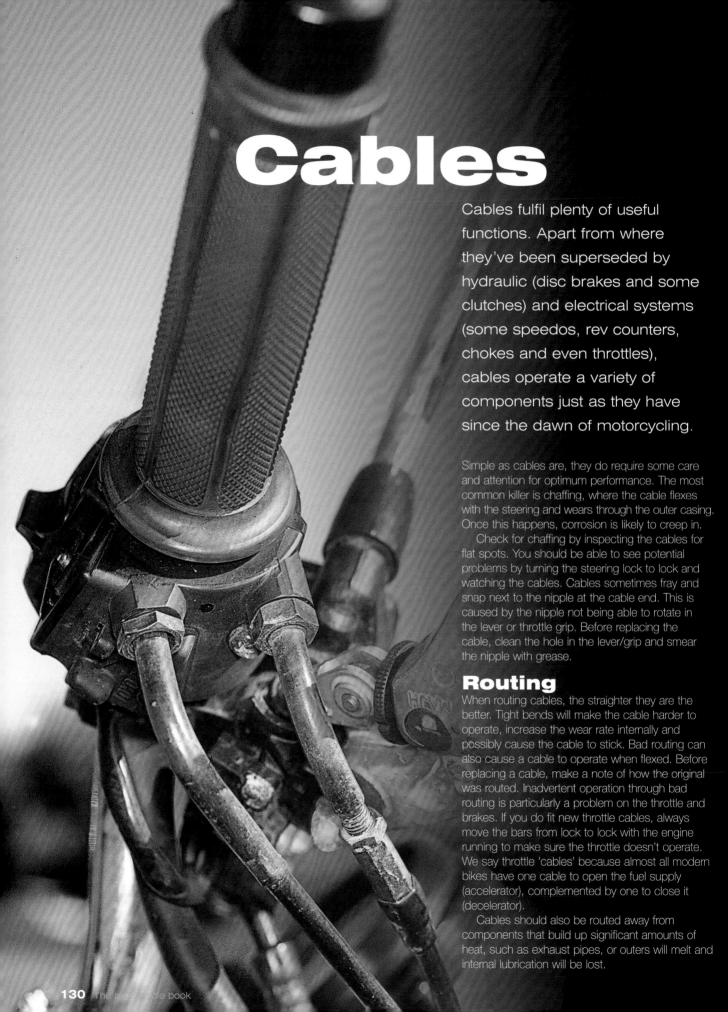

Cables

Cables fulfil plenty of useful functions. Apart from where they've been superseded by hydraulic (disc brakes and some clutches) and electrical systems (some speedos, rev counters, chokes and even throttles), cables operate a variety of components just as they have since the dawn of motorcycling.

Simple as cables are, they do require some care and attention for optimum performance. The most common killer is chaffing, where the cable flexes with the steering and wears through the outer casing. Once this happens, corrosion is likely to creep in.

Check for chaffing by inspecting the cables for flat spots. You should be able to see potential problems by turning the steering lock to lock and watching the cables. Cables sometimes fray and snap next to the nipple at the cable end. This is caused by the nipple not being able to rotate in the lever or throttle grip. Before replacing the cable, clean the hole in the lever/grip and smear the nipple with grease.

Routing

When routing cables, the straighter they are the better. Tight bends will make the cable harder to operate, increase the wear rate internally and possibly cause the cable to stick. Bad routing can also cause a cable to operate when flexed. Before replacing a cable, make a note of how the original was routed. Inadvertent operation through bad routing is particularly a problem on the throttle and brakes. If you do fit new throttle cables, always move the bars from lock to lock with the engine running to make sure the throttle doesn't operate. We say throttle 'cables' because almost all modern bikes have one cable to open the fuel supply (accelerator), complemented by one to close it (decelerator).

Cables should also be routed away from components that build up significant amounts of heat, such as exhaust pipes, or outers will melt and internal lubrication will be lost.

Free play on this R1's accelerator and decelerator cables is measured at the throttle itself. Too much or too little, and the cables will have to be adjusted.

Adjustments are made here by pulling the cable outer from the adjuster body. Adjuster and locknut can be seen clearly.

Here are the coarse adjusters at the carburettor end. When fitting cables it's best to take all the adjustment out of the fine adjusters and set the cables up using these coarse adjusters. Then as the cables stretch, the fine adjusters can be used to take up the slack.

Adjustment

Cables must be correctly adjusted for proper operation of controls. There must be adequate free play between the inner and outer so that controls aren't inadvertently operated when the bars are turned or the suspension extends and compresses. For correct cable adjustment, refer to your manual. Most are adjusted by simple barrel and locknut arrangements. In the case of cable clutches and front brakes, it is done by knurled wheel adjusters at the lever end for fine adjustment (as the cable stretches slightly in use), and other adjusters at the gearbox or brake end for coarser adjustment. Some throttle cables have fine adjusters near the twistgrip and coarser ones at the carb/throttle body end too.

Lubrication

As cables get older they get harder to use. This can be caused by fraying of the internal wire, or by dirt build up in the cable. If a cable is frayed, then it should be replaced immediately. If it is simply dirty, then lubricating the cable might displace some of the dirt and also make it easier to use.

It is possible to lubricate cables by creating a reservoir at one end and letting gravity draw lubricant through the cable. A quicker method is to use force. For less than £10, you can buy an adaptor that seals itself around one end of a cable. You then connect an aerosol lubricant (not chain lube) and squirt. The pressure expels dirt and ensures the cable is fully lubricated.

An alternative method is to use a pressure lubricator that is filled with light oil and operated by hand to force the oil through the cable. If an inner cable has a nylon liner, don't use oil to lubricate it. Oil can make the liner swell, and cause the cable to seize. Use a silicone spray instead.

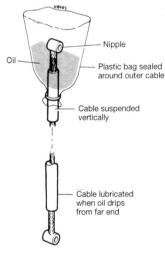

Nipple

Oil

Plastic bag sealed around outer cable

Cable suspended vertically

Cable lubricated when oil drips from far end

Home-brewed cable lubricator (above). Pressure lubricator (far left) makes the job quick and easy, as does aerosol adaptor (left).

Without oil, engines will do considerable harm to themselves and won't run for long. Oil prevents damage by separating surfaces with a thin film, allowing parts to move past each other with minimal wear or friction.

Oil and filter change

Changing oil is easier on a warm engine because the oil is thinner. Remove the filler first to let the old lube flow more freely.

When removing the oil drain-plug, watch out for the initial gush of hot oil – and for other hot components, such as exhaust pipes. Make sure the drain tray you have under the sump is large enough to hold the used lube.

When fitting a filter, smear a small amount of clean oil evenly around the rubber seal and make sure no dirt has dropped on to the sealing face.

Fill the engine to the correct level with the bike upright – you'll get a false reading if the bike's on its side stand. It's important to use the right grade of engine oil, as specified by the manufacturer, so check your manual.

To top up the engine oil, wipe the oil level inspection window, located on the right-hand side of the engine, so that it is clean. With the motorcycle vertical, the oil level should lie between the maximum and minimum levels on the window. If the level is below the minimum line, remove the filler cap from the top of the clutch cover. Top the engine up with the recommended grade and type of oil, to bring the level up to the maximum level on the window. Re-install the filler cap.

A large part of oil's role is a clean-up job in the motor. Over a period of time, an engine's oil will become contaminated with by-products of the combustion process, including unburnt fuel, moisture from condensation and even coolant from the water jacket. All of this degrades its performance. These problems are on top of the degradation of the lubricant as it performs its basic job of cooling and lubing. Shearing forces break up the oil's molecular structure as it works hard to prevent the engine's key components from grinding themselves to bits, which is exactly what bits of metal flinging themselves at each other several thousands times a minute would inevitably do.

Use the recommended oil for your bike as specified by the manufacturer. Your bike was designed to run with mineral, semi-synthetic or fully-synthetic oil. If you wish to upgrade, check with the bike's manufacturer or importer. Using the wrong oil can lead to clutch slip or worse. Don't be tempted to use cheap car oil of apparently the same spec. If you're unsure of what oil a second-hand bike's been filled with, drain and refill with semi-synthetic. You can go either way from there, depending on what's specified for the bike.

Making the change

Changing a bike's oil involves replacing the oil and filter. It's a good idea to replace them together, or at least fit a new filter every other oil change. Clogged filters can do as much damage as no oil, since they impede correct flow of lubricant, and fitting new filters without changing old oil won't improve the lube's performance.

Most bikes over 125cc have filters. Locations vary but are usually low down on the front or side of the engine for external filters, and underneath for internal ones. Nearly all external filters screw on. There are a number of strap and socket-drive tools available to remove them, and although it works,

stabbing them with a screwdriver is best avoided – as anyone who's had an eyeful of hot oil can testify. Replace filters with genuine bike manufacturer parts, or parts of the correct specification.

When disposing of used oil, it's your moral – and indeed legal – duty to dispose of it correctly. The drain by the back door won't do. Transfer the contents of the oil drain can into the tin your new oil came in, and then take it to the local authority dump, where they'll know what to do with it.

Most modern sump drain-plugs have a magnetic end to catch small pieces of swarf generated by internal engine friction. These plugs should be wiped clean before refitting. It's also advisable to replace the sealing washer with a new one. These are often copper, or another soft metal such as aluminium, and sometimes they have a rubber insert. It's easy to be tempted to turn the washer upside down, assuming it will do the same job as a new one. But this ruse rarely works more than once, and what might start as a messy trickle can quickly turn into a messy and dangerous deluge if the sump plug decides to let go.

When first starting the bike after an oil refill, don't over rev it. It takes a while to fill the filter and build pressure in the system. Until then, you're relying on the oil film on components keeping the key parts safe, so give them an easy time. If the oil pressure warning light doesn't go out after a few seconds, stop the engine immediately. The problem might be down to a multitude of reasons after an engine rebuild. But after a refill, it's more likely to be because of adding too little oil or a major leak from filter or drain-plug – you did remember to refit them, didn't you? We only ask because it's all too easy to forget – and then fail to notice the spreading puddle of fresh lube on the garage floor before realising there is a problem. So never conduct maintenance in a rush. Let the bike idle for a few minutes, before rechecking the oil level.

Oil drain cans/trays sold in car accessory shops are large enough to hold the contents of any bike sump.

Socket wrench driven tool for easy removal of external spin-on oil filters.

Cooling systems

Engines are not very efficient. Most of the energy released during combustion is transferred into heat and escapes into the engine or down the exhaust pipe. All the heat building up in the engine has to go somewhere, or the bike will overheat and the engine will be damaged. That's where cooling comes in.

Engines are either air-cooled or liquid-cooled. Liquid-cooling is the most popular choice these days, but is also more complicated. Air-cooled engines are very straightforward. The flow of air over the engine, as the bike moves along, takes the heat with it. Barrels and heads have deep horizontal fins to help with heat dissipation. Problems only arise in very hot climates or if the machine is static or moving slowly for long periods. Some air-cooled bikes have oil-coolers, which look like radiators, to help the lubricant play a more efficient role in taking heat away from the engine. The old Suzuki GSX engines, as still used in the Bandit, are a good example of this. Suzuki describes them as air/oil-cooled.

In a liquid-cooled engine, coolant is pumped through a network of drillings in the motor's castings. Heat transfers to the coolant which then passes through a radiator where it is cooled. If for any reason the coolant doesn't flow, the engine will overheat.

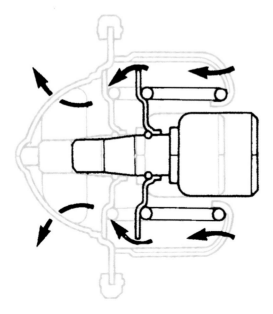

The thermostat lets the engine get up to temperature before opening to allow the coolant to flow to the radiator.

Thermostats

A thermostat in the system gauges when the coolant is up to operating temperature and then allows it to flow to the radiator and the rest of the system. If it wasn't there, the bike would take a long time to warm up. If it fails to open, the engine will overheat. If you suspect the thermostat is faulty, it must be checked. If it is open at room temperature, then it has failed and must be replaced. To test that it opens, heat it in a pan of water and, using a thermometer, check the temperature at which it opens and compare the figure with the spec in your manual. Also check the amount it stays open after being heated at 90ºC for a few minutes and, again, compare this figure with the specifications in your manual.

Temperature sensors

These are mounted in the engine block or cylinder head and are electrical devices whose resistance falls as coolant temperature rises. One brings the electric fan or fans behind the radiator into operation, while another is connected to the temperature gauge on your instrument cluster. On some models, one sensor combines these two operations.

If the fan stays on all the time, doesn't come on at all or cuts in at the wrong temperature, suspect the fan sensor (having first checked the fuse, if the fan doesn't operate at all). Likewise, if the temperature gauge doesn't work or gives clearly inappropriate readings, suspect the sensor.

Both of these sensors can be tested, but the procedure is more complex than for thermostats. See your manual.

Coolant

The most common problem with liquid-cooled engines is lack of coolant. Check the coolant is between the high and low levels on the expansion tank. Don't overfill the system because it has to vent as the liquid expands. Be sure to top up with the correct coolant for your bike.

Leaks reduce a system's effectiveness because coolant can escape and the system doesn't pressurise, reducing the coolant's boiling point. Check hoses and joints for leakage and inspect the radiator too. Sometimes leaks occur internally in the engine for various reasons and these are more serious. Coolant in the oil, which leads to a deposit that looks like mayonnaise, or oil in the coolant is a sign of this.

If the radiator fins have become clogged externally with road dirt or the odd unfortunate pigeon, air can't pass through it and the engine will run hot. Clean it using water from a hose in the opposite direction to which air flows, or, with care, a compressed air line.

Cooling systems are sometimes blocked by corrosion carried into the radiator. Although you can use water (distilled is far better than tap) in cooling systems, it's far better to use dedicated coolant or anti-freeze of the correct type for your bike as both have corrosion inhibitors. Anti-freeze also protects the system during cold weather. Plain water or coolant without anti-freeze can turn into ice, which may lead to cracks in the system. When topping up a system filled with anti-freeze, don't use just water on its own as this will dilute the anti-freeze, lessening its efficiency. For maximum protection, coolant should be replaced every two years, although some systems are sealed for life.

Draining and refilling the cooling system

This is normally done in two stages and must always be done with the engine cold. Remove the pressure cap on the radiator to help the system drain. This must never be removed with the engine hot since scalding coolant and steam may escape and cause injury. When you're sure the engine is cool, remove the cap carefully and slowly with a rag over it. Remember that cooling systems are pressurised and there may still be enough pressure to spit coolant out at you.

Disconnect the hose from the neck of the radiator and use it to empty the expansion tank into a container sufficiently large to hold all the coolant in your bike's system. If any old coolant remains in the expansion tank, remove the tank and tip the fluid out. Next, loosen and remove the lowest coolant hose you can see on the engine. This should drain the radiator and engine. Often there are other drain plugs on the cylinder block and water pump cover. Remove these as well to allow any remaining coolant to escape.

Old coolant must be disposed of carefully, so check with your local authority to find out the location of the nearest dump who can deal with it. Never leave it lying around. It's highly toxic so keep it away from children and animals. Wipe up any spills. Anti-freeze is inflammable as well.

Refill the system, being careful to check for air by squeezing rubber hoses and possibly bleeding the pump if required. Check your manual for the complete procedure for your bike. Remember to fill the expansion tank to the correct level too.

The reservoir is usually mounted on the right-hand end of the radiator. Check that the coolant level is between the 'FULL' and 'LOW' level lines marked on the reservoir.

If the coolant level is low, remove any bodywork obstructing the filler cap. Remove the cap and top up the coolant with the recommended coolant mixture. Fit the cap securely. Then re-install any bodywork.

Bearings

Compared to the engine, a bike's chassis is relatively free of bearings. But chassis bearings require more care than any in the engine, which have a ready supply of warm lubricant to look after them. There are four sets of chassis bearings to check – wheel, swingarm, rear suspension linkages and bushes, and headstock.

The wheel and headstock bearings are perhaps the most important. They're certainly the ones most capable of adversely affecting the handling characteristics. However, checking them is a fairly simple task, especially with a friend helping.

Wheel bearings

To check the front wheel bearings, you need to establish if there is any sideplay. The wheel should be free to spin forwards and backwards. To check bearings, set the steering in the straight ahead position. If you don't have a front paddock stand, ask a friend to lean the bike on its side stand until the front is off the ground. Things are even easier if your bike is equipped with a centre stand – have your helper lean on the back of the bike.

Grab the wheel from one side and try pulling the top towards you while pushing the bottom end away. Any clicking or clunking is likely to be in the bearings, and the wheel should be removed to replace them. The procedure is the same for the rear wheel, and again it's easier if the wheel is off the ground by means of a paddock stand, centre stand (where fitted), or your ever-helpful mate pulling the bike over on its sidestand.

Wheel bearings are usually the ball type, with one pressed into each side of the hub. Chain-drive bikes often have a third bearing in the cush/sprocket carrier assembly of the rear wheel. It's a similar deal with shaft-drive bikes, which often have an additional bearing or bearings in the bevel mechanism for the shaft drive. See your manual for bearing replacement procedure.

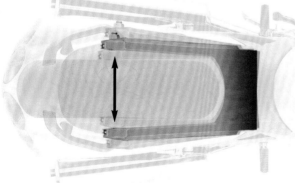

Swingarm bearings
As with most bearings, the swingarm's bearings or bushes are easiest checked with the help of a friend.

Wheel Bearings
Side-to-side wheel play or roughness when the wheel is rotated means the bearings are shot.

Swingarm & rear suspension bearings

On bikes with greasing points for these bearings, their life can be considerably lengthened by lubricating as per the maintenance schedule in your manual.

Checking the swingarm pivot bearings is a similar procedure to wheel bearings, but you won't be able to check them on a paddock stand because you need to try to move the swingarm from side-to-side. Use the mate and side stand trick. If the bearings feel suspect, you can carry out the same test with the suspension disconnected from the swingarm. To do this, though, the bike will have to be on a centre stand or stand under the engine or suspended from a beam in the workshop. It's much easier to feel swingarm pivot bearing play this way.

Swingarm bearings will either be bushes or needle, taper or ball roller type. Sometimes there's a combination of types. Refer to your manual for details on replacement.

The suspension linkage on monoshock bikes carries bushes or needle roller or ball bearings. To check for play in these, the rear wheel has to be off the floor with no weight on the swingarm. Grab the top of the rear wheel and pull it upwards. There should be no clunk or free play. Again, refer to your manual for details on replacement.

Steering bearings

Headstock, or steering, bearings need to be checked in two ways. With no weight on the front wheel (time to call on that mate again), move the bars left to right. On models fitted with a steering damper, make sure the damper is backed off to the position of least resistance. Steering action should be smooth and light. Any notchiness or tight spots are signs of bearing damage, and they should be replaced.

Because of the hammering these bearings get, they often work loose. Still with no weight on the front, get someone to push and pull quite hard on the bottom of the fork legs. While they do this, check for small movement by placing your fingers between the back of the top yoke and front of the tank. If you feel movement, the bearings are loose and need adjusting, the procedure for which will be in your manual.

Steering bearings benefit from regular regreasing and being correctly adjusted. The main types these days are taper roller and caged ball, although a few, mainly smaller, bikes still use uncaged balls. These are a laugh-a-minute to fit, since the grease you've used to hold them in the bottom race, while you get the bottom yoke back in, fails to do so, and the tiny balls drop on to the workshop floor.

Bearing markings reveal the bearing type. It can be a lot cheaper to buy from a specialist bearing shop.

Rear suspension bearings and bushes These must be checked with the wheel off the ground and no weight on the swingarm.

Steering head bearings These need to be checked for side-to-side and front-to-back movement. Good handling relies on chassis bearings being in good condition and properly lubed and adjusted.

Electrical

Electrical systems are the most common cause of problems on bikes, so it pays to keep on top of them. Modern bike electrics are becoming increasingly complex but also increasingly robust, making the bikes we ride more reliable at the same time. Just a little bit of care will keep them that way.

Battery
Doesn't last forever, but keep topped-up, with de-ionised water, between the lines so the plates in each cell are covered in non-sealed types. Watch out for build up of clag at the bottom of cells.

Battery

The obvious place to start is the battery. Unless you've got a modern sealed battery, you need to check it's filled to within the correct levels as indicated on the casing. If low, top it up with a little de-ionised water, but be careful not to get any acidic fluid from the battery on you or your clothes (or the bike). A battery that needs to be topped up too regularly indicates problems with the charging system. Refer to your manual for checks.

It is also well worth ensuring that the battery terminals are tight. These can work loose and cause problems that are hard to trace. A splodge of petroleum jelly or battery grease prevents corrosion forming on the terminals and ensures a good connection.

Typically, a conventional lead acid battery will last for up to three years, provided it is properly maintained and kept charged up when the bike isn't in regular use.

Connectors

Satisfied that the battery is in good condition, it's worth checking the push-fit connectors that link the various electrical components. You'll find these all over most bikes, and if moisture gets in, it can cause failures. Split the connections and spray a little contact cleaner on the pins. Be careful not to spray bodywork or other plastic or painted components since they may be attacked by the contact cleaner.

Smearing a little bit of silicon grease or a squirt of WD40 on the connector body will make them easier to split next time.

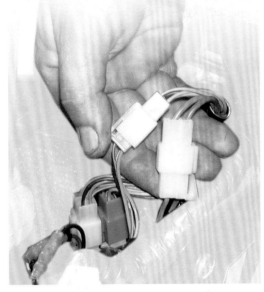

Connectors
A little bit of preventative maintenance will ensure they keep the electricity flowing to where it needs to go.

Bulbs

Check that your lights work. That might sound simple but it's amazing how easy it is to forget this. It makes good sense before every ride to check head and tail lights, indicators and to apply both brakes to check the brake light and its switches are working – and there are probably some meticulous souls that do. At the other end of the spectrum, there are riders who need to be told their rear light has failed and only notice headlight problems when they can't see in the dark. But it pays to be less slack than this because there is a major safety issue here.

Some bikes seem to get through rear bulbs at an alarming rate. This is often caused by vibration, so make sure the light unit is fitted correctly.

If you notice the direction indicator idiot light on the dash flashing quicker than usual, it's normally a sign one or more of the indicator bulbs have failed.

When performing your routine checks of lights and indicators, give the horn a quick blast to make sure that's working too.

Bulbs do blow now and again, but usually through old age and sometimes vibration. If they persistently fail, there's a problem.

Fuses

The first thing to suspect when an electrical component stops working is its fuse. Bike fuse boxes are usually located in easily accessible places – under the seat, side panel or inboard of the fairing.

There's usually a helpful key on a printed label in the lid of the fuse box to tell you which does what, and sometimes there's a couple of spares too. Some smaller machines just have a single fuse for all the systems, usually found near the battery.

A blown fuse often indicates a short circuit or a faulty electrical component, but sometimes they just blow for no reason, especially on bikes that vibrate a lot. If you replace a fuse and it blows again, the fault requires further investigation. Time to get the manual out. Some bikes use a resettable circuit breaker in place of the main fuse.

Fuses protect key components from electrical overload damage. Sometimes they just fail. Immediate failure on replacement shows there's a more serious fault.

Blown

Un-blown

Switches

Handlebar switches are probably the most exposed electrical components – particularly on unfaired bikes. It is a good idea, once a year, to remove the switches, scrape away the corrosion, chase out the spiders, and apply a light smear of petroleum jelly to the switch components – metal and plastic.

A couple more tips

If you use a pressure washer to clean your bike, be careful not to blast electrical connectors or components. Although most systems are designed to be watertight, the force from a pressure washer may be too much.

Side stand kill-switches often get covered in chain lube from the front sprocket. Because they have the ability to kill the ignition system, keep them clean. Don't use solvent cleaners; simply wipe them with a rag and check that they operate freely and smoothly.

MoTs

An MoT certificate is simply a bit of paper stating that a particular bike was in roadworthy condition at the time it was inspected. It's also a legal requirement – every bike over three years old used on the road in the UK has to have one. You can't buy a tax disc without it and your insurance may be invalidated if you have an accident while your bike has no MoT. Here are the areas the MoT inspector will be looking at. You'll save a lot of time and hassle if you look at them yourself before going to the test centre.

Brakes

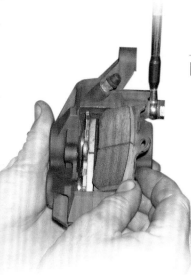

- ▶ Each wheel will be raised off the ground, the brakes operated then released and the wheel spun to check for binding.

- ▶ Brake discs will be checked for cracks and to ensure they're securely mounted.

- ▶ Pad material will be checked visually on disc systems to ensure the pads aren't on their wear limit.

- ▶ Drum brakes will be checked for correct operation of the lever and that the angle between operating cable or rod and the lever on the brake drum isn't too large with the brake applied.

- ▶ Brake hoses and their unions will be looked at for bulging in flexible pipes, and signs of corrosion and hydraulic fluid leakage elsewhere.

- ▶ Rear brake torque arms will be checked for security and that fasteners are held on by locknuts or split pins.

- ▶ ABS-equipped bikes have a self-check warning light in the instrument cluster, and the tester will check that this is working.

- ▶ The tester will check braking efficiency, but this is nothing to worry about if you're satisfied your brakes are properly maintained.

Steering

- ▶ The front wheel will be raised off the ground and the bars turned from lock to lock to check bars and switches don't foul the tank or trap the rider's thumbs. Busted lockstops and poorly fitted non-standard bars can cause problems here.

- ▶ At the same time, the tester will be looking for free steering movement without drag or notchiness caused by incorrectly routed cables or worn or badly adjusted head bearings.

- ▶ The tester will look for play in the head bearings by pulling on the bottom of the fork legs.

- ▶ Handlebars and controls must be securely mounted, as must the grips.

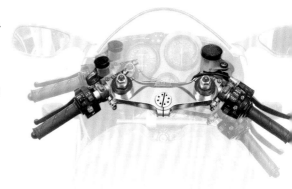

Wheels and tyres

▸ Cast wheels must be free from cracks. Spoked wheels must have a full complement of spokes, free from corrosion, unbent and correctly tensioned.

▸ Rims must be uncreased and true. Wheels will be raised from the ground and spun to check for truth of tyres and rims, and also to make sure they don't foul mudguards, huggers or suspension components.

▸ Wheel bearings will be checked for excessive wear. See the pages in this chapter on bearings for advice on how to check these.

▸ Tyres will be checked for adequate tread and sidewall, and tread condition. See the section on tyres for more information on this.

▸ Tyres will also be checked to ensure they are of the correct type and match each other front and rear. Tyres must be suitable for road use. Anything marked otherwise will fail the MoT, so hand-cut slicks are out. Direction arrows on the tyres will be checked too.

▸ Security of wheel spindles is another item on the tester's agenda. Where they were fitted as standard, self-locking or castellated nuts with split or R-clips must still be present.

▸ Wheel alignment will also be checked. You can do this yourself by referring to this chapter's section on chains.

Final drive

▸ Chains and belts must be in good condition and at the correct tension. The rear wheel sprocket must be securely mounted on the hub. The overall condition of the sprocket will be checked too.

▸ On shafties, the bevel unit will be checked for leaks that could lead to oil getting on to the rear tyre.

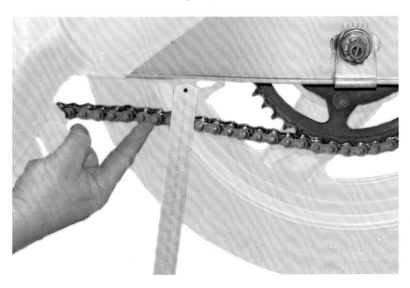

General checks

▶ Remember, the MoT tester isn't looking to catch you out. He's simply checking that your bike is roadworthy and therefore safe. So apart from the items detailed above, check that body panels, seat, mudguard fairings and major fasteners are secure.

▶ All footrests and controls must be securely mounted. Excessive corrosion on the frame or load-bearing components will result in a fail, so check these areas too.

▶ Finally, make sure your bike is presentable. If you wheel it through the door with parts wired on and broken bits dragging on the floor, it's likely you'll be asked to wheel it straight out again. The better the general condition of the bike, the better your chances of an MoT pass.

Exhaust

▶ It must be securely mounted and not fouling rear suspension components.

▶ The bike will be started and the throttle operated to ensure there are no holes or leaks in the entire system, including the collector box, where applicable.

▶ The tester will look for either an original fitment end-can, or the BSAU 193 stamp on the silencer. Bikes made before 1 January 1985 are exempt from this requirement. Anything marked 'race use only' or 'not for road use' will be failed. Overall loudness of questionable cans and systems generally is at the tester's discretion.

Rear suspension

▶ The inspector will have an assistant hold the front of the bike while he or she bounces the rear with the bike off its stand. The inspector is looking for adequate damping in the rear shock(s) while checking nothing is being fouled.

▶ The inspector will look at the shock(s) to check the damper rod(s) aren't corroding and the damping oil isn't leaking.

▶ The swingarm's pivot bearings will be checked, with the rear wheel raised off the ground, by pulling it from side-to-side. At the same time, the rear wheel will be pulled up by its highest point to check for wear in the suspension linkages.

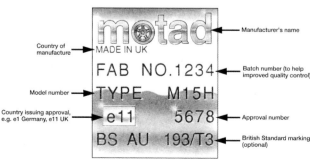

Country of manufacture → MADE IN UK
Manufacturer's name → motad
Batch number (to help improved quality control) → FAB NO.1234
Model number → TYPE M15H
Country issuing approval, e.g. e1 Germany, e11 UK → e11 5678
Approval number →
British Standard marking (optional) → BS AU 193/T3

Lights, indicators, horn and reflector

▸ Headlight and tail light must both operate with the switch in high and low beam positions.

▸ With the switch in the parking light position, the front and tail lights must light up.

▸ Indicators must flash at the proper speed and the idiot lights and switch must work properly. If your bike has a hazard warning system, all four indicators must flash when it's operated.

▸ The brake light must come on when each brake is operated. Bikes after 1 April 1986 must have a brake light switch for both front and rear brakes.

▸ The horn must have a continuous tone and sufficient volume.

▸ The headlight beam must be at the right height. The MoT station has equipment to check this. If you think yours is out, check it as per the diagram on this page. Draw a horizontal line on the garage wall at the same height as the centre of your headlight and position the bike as per the distance and angle shown in the diagram. Draw a vertical mark in line with the centreline of the bike. Now take the bike off its stand and sit on it. When the headlight is dipped, the beam on the wall should fall below the horizontal and to the left of the vertical lines.

Front suspension

▸ With the bike off the stand, the tester will sit on it, hold the front brake on and pump the forks up and down to check they don't bind and there's adequate damping.

▸ Fork seals and the stanchion area next to them will be checked, the former for leaks and the latter for pitting or corrosion.

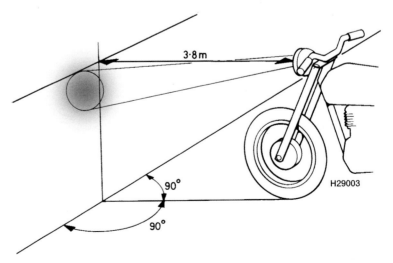

3·8 m

90°

90°

H29003

Storage

Unless you're commuting to and from work on your bike, it will probably spend a few months of the year in storage. But storing a bike isn't just a case of putting it in the shed and forgetting about it – not if you want it to be in a decent state when summer returns.

Motorcycles are highly susceptible to corrosion caused by road salt, because their parts are so exposed. Corrosion can start in a matter of days, and is hard to halt. So give the bike a good wash before you put it away, and make sure it's completely dry before it's consigned to the shed.

If the bike is faired, remove the fairing to reach the awkward places underneath. A firm-bristled bottle brush makes life easier and saves your knuckles, although using a pressure washer is perhaps the most convenient and effective method. Just remember not to be too vigorous around steering, suspension and wheel bearings, and electrical components. Lube the chain afterwards too.

Coat the piston bores and rings with oil by removing the spark plugs and squirting around a teaspoon of oil down each spark plug hole. Put the plugs back in and crank the engine over with the kickstart (where fitted), or on the electric start with the kill-switch off. Some bikes only allow the engine to turn with the kill-switch on so the plugs will have to be earthed against the cylinder head – far enough away from the spark plug holes to avoid igniting any fuel vapour in the bores.

Consider draining the petrol or, at the very least, turn the fuel tap off and run the bike until it stops. This prevents petrol residue building up in the carbs and blocking small orifices. Otherwise, turn off the fuel tap and drain the carbs by way of the drain screws at the bottom of the float bowls. If your bike is going to be off the road for a long time, you might want to add fuel stabiliser to the petrol. Otherwise, petrol can go off in storage and you'll need to replace it come springtime. Remember to dispose of old fuel properly.

Completely drained tanks can corrode internally if left for a long time. Remove the tank, pour half a litre of engine oil into it and agitate the tank to coat the inside with oil. Remember to clean the oil out before refilling the tank with petrol. Alternatively, spray the inside of the tank with WD40 or similar.

Air intakes and silencer orifices can be plugged or covered in polythene to prevent build up of condensation. Run the bike until it's hot, allow to cool, then cover.

Most batteries, even new ones, will discharge if the bike is unused over the winter. The problem is worse if the bike is alarmed, no matter how small the drain. A trickle charger helps keep batteries topped up, without damaging them. It's best to remove the battery from the bike and keep it in a place where there's no danger of it freezing.

If it's an unsealed type, ensure there's enough electrolyte in it.

If the bike is liquid-cooled, check it has anti-freeze in. It takes only one freezing night to do expensive damage. Corrosion inhibitors in the anti-freeze will help prevent internal damage to the cooling system. And if the bike is chain driven, make sure it's lubed – a rusty chain wears faster. While lubing, you might consider a light coat of WD40 or

similar on the wheel rims if they're chrome, and on fork sliders and other exposed metal parts. Remember not to spray the brake discs however.

Finally, check tyre pressures. A bike stood for several months on flat tyres is likely to deform them so badly that they lose their shape, or even worse, develop splits. Deflate by no more than 5–10psi. If your bike has a centre stand, put it on that with blocks of wood under each wheel to save them from damp. If possible, store the bike on paddock stands so that the wheels are off the ground. If you haven't got any such stands, rotate the wheels periodically so they're not standing on the same section of tyre.

Tempting as it is to start the engine every so often, try not to unless you intend to let it get up to operating temperature. If the engine isn't thoroughly warm, condensation is likely to form in the engine and contaminate the oil, possibly causing internal corrosion.

Trickle chargers keep batteries in optimum condition.

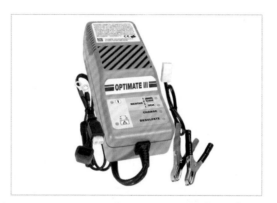

Disconnect the battery while your bike's in storage.

If a cable-operated clutch sticks in storage, tie the lever back to see if it frees.

Is your bike **legal?**

Numberplate

It was popular over the past few years, for aesthetic reasons, to replace the standard numberplate on sportsbikes with a smaller one. However, the law is specific about numberplates and requires them to be a certain size, with letters of a certain size and spacing. Anything else is illegal, and will probably get you stopped.

Exhaust pipe

Aftermarket exhaust cans are the most popular thing people fit, either because they want the extra noise and performance, or simply because after a crash it's a cheaper alternative to buying a replacement stock silencer. However, unless the exhaust meets Government noise requirements and is marked to say so, it is illegal for road use. Most race cans have a 'not for road use' marking and removing this doesn't make it legal.

Headlight cover

The law says forward-facing lights should be white and rear-facing lights should be red. Any departure from this is illegal. Headlight covers are often fitted to colour match with the bodywork. These are illegal. Clear covers are useful because they prevent costly stone damage to the headlight.

Bigger tyres

Although not illegal, fitting larger or smaller tyres than those recommended by the manufacturer is inadvisable. More than anything, it will affect the bike's handling, and there's a chance your insurance company could use it as an excuse not to pay out in an accident.

Paintwork

There is no law against what colour your bike can be, although you couldn't get away with having it painted like a police bike. It's generally frowned upon to have race-like numbers on it.

Pillions

So long as the bike was designed to take pillions, and so long as the person riding pillion can sit with their feet on the pegs, it's okay for them to ride pillion. The only real legal requirements are that they wear a helmet and that you're licensed to carry them. Some insurance policies exclude cover for pillions, so it's worth checking your own policy.

Trouble
shooting

When things go wrong, as they sometimes do, don't panic. A motorcycle is a mechanical entity and as such is governed by rules of basic engineering and mechanics. By applying a little logic it's reasonably easy to drill down to the root of a problem, and even if your own mechanical skills or workshop resources don't stretch to it, you'll be able to point the guys in the shop in the right direction.

To help you see the trees from the forest, there follows some basic fault-finding material which will at least guide you in the right direction. Two-stroke riders can ignore any references to valves and camshafts, of course, but the rest of the material pretty much applies regardless of engine type. Remember this is a general guide, so for specific treatment of problems refer to the Haynes manual for your bike.

Engine doesn't start or is difficult to start

Starter motor doesn't rotate

Engine kill switch OFF.
Fuse blown. Check main fuse and starter circuit fuse. See your Haynes manual.

Battery voltage low.
Check and recharge battery.

Starter motor defective.
Make sure the wiring to the starter is secure. Make sure the starter relay clicks when the start button is pushed. If the relay clicks, then the fault is in the wiring or motor.

Starter relay faulty.
See your Haynes manual.

Starter switch not contacting.
The contacts could be wet, corroded or dirty. Disassemble and clean the switch. See your Haynes manual.

Wiring open or shorted.
Check all wiring connections and harnesses to make sure that they are dry, tight and not corroded. Also check for broken or frayed wires that can cause a short to ground (earth). Refer to the wiring diagram in your Haynes manual.

Ignition (main) switch defective.
Check the switch according to the procedure in your Haynes manual. Replace the switch with a new one if it is defective.

Engine kill switch defective.
Check for wet, dirty or corroded contacts. Clean or replace the switch as necessary.

Faulty neutral, side stand or clutch switch.
Check the wiring to each switch and the switch itself according to the procedures in your Haynes manual.

Starter motor rotates but engine does not turn over

Starter clutch defective.
Inspect and repair or replace. See your Haynes manual.

Damaged idle/reduction or starter gears.
Inspect and replace the damaged parts. See your Haynes manual.

Starter works but engine won't turn over (seized).
Seized engine caused by one or more internally damaged components. Failure due to wear, abuse or lack of lubrication. Damage can include seized valves, followers, camshafts, pistons, crankshaft, connecting rod bearings, or transmission gears or bearings. See your Haynes manual for engine disassembly.

No fuel flow

No fuel in tank.

Fuel tank breather hose obstructed.

Fuel tap filter or in-line filter (carburettor models) or fuel pump assembly filter (fuel injection models) clogged.
Remove the tap or pump and clean or renew the filter. See your Haynes manual.

Fuel line clogged.
Pull the fuel line loose and carefully blow it through.

Float needle valve clogged (carburettor models).
For all of the valves to be clogged, either a very bad batch of fuel with an unusual additive has been used, or some other foreign material has entered the tank. Many times after a machine has been stored for many months without running, the fuel turns to a varnish-like liquid and forms deposits on the inlet needle valves and jets. The carburettors should be removed and overhauled if draining the float chambers doesn't solve the problem.

Fuel pump or relay (fuel injection models) faulty.
Check the fuel pump and relay. See your Haynes manual.

Engine flooded (carburettor models).
Float height too high. Check as described in your Haynes manual.

Float needle valve worn or stuck open.
Dirt, rust or other debris can cause the valve to seat improperly, causing excess fuel to be admitted to the float chamber. In this case, the float chamber should be cleaned and the needle valve and seat inspected. If the needle and seat are worn, then the leaking will persist and the parts should be replaced.

Starting technique incorrect.
Under normal circumstances (i.e. if all the carburettor functions are sound) the machine should start with little or no throttle. When the engine is cold, the choke should be operated and the engine started without opening the throttle. When the engine is at operating temperature, only a very slight amount of throttle should be necessary. If the engine is flooded, turn the fuel tap OFF (where fitted) and hold the throttle open while cranking the engine. This will allow additional air to reach the cylinders. Remember to turn the fuel tap back ON after the engine starts.

Engine flooded (fuel injection models).
Faulty pressure regulator – if it is stuck closed there could be excessive pressure in the fuel rail. Check as described in your Haynes manual.

Injector(s) stuck open, allowing a constant flow of fuel into the engine.
Check as described in your Haynes manual.

Starting technique incorrect.
See advice as for carburated bikes. But remember some fuel injected bikes have no choke lever and most have no manually-operated fuel tap.

No spark or weak spark

Ignition switch OFF.

Engine kill switch turned to the OFF position.

Battery voltage low.
Check and recharge the battery as necessary. See your Haynes manual.

Spark plugs dirty, defective or worn out.
Locate reason for fouled plugs using spark plug condition chart and follow the plug maintenance procedures. See your Haynes manual.

Spark plug caps faulty.
Check condition. Replace if cracks or deterioration are evident. See your Haynes manual.

Spark plug caps not making good contact.
Make sure that the plug caps fit snugly over the plug ends.

Ignition control unit (carburettor models) or ECM (fuel injection models) defective.
Check the unit, referring to your Haynes manual for details.

Pulse generator defective.
Check the unit, referring to your Haynes manual for details.

Ignition coils defective.
Check the coils, referring to your Haynes manual.

Ignition or kill switch shorted.
Usually caused by water, corrosion, damage or excessive wear. The switches can be disassembled and cleaned with electrical contact cleaner. If cleaning does not help, replace the switches referring to your Haynes manual.

Wiring shorted or broken between:
a) Ignition (main) switch and engine kill switch (or blown fuse)
b) Ignition control unit or ECM and engine kill switch
c) Ignition control unit or ECM and ignition coils
d) Ignition coils and spark plugs
e) Ignition control unit or ECM and pulse generator.

Make sure that all wiring connections are clean, dry and tight.
Look for chafed and broken wires.

Compression low

Spark plugs loose.
Remove the plugs and inspect their threads. Reinstall and tighten to the specified torque. See your Haynes manual.

Cylinder heads not sufficiently tightened down.
See your Haynes manual. If a cylinder head is suspected of being loose, then there's a chance that the gasket or head is damaged if the problem has persisted for any length of time.

Incorrect valve clearance.
Check and adjust the valve clearances as per your manual.

Cylinder and/or piston worn.
Excessive wear will cause compression pressure to leak past the rings. This is usually accompanied by worn rings as well. A top-end overhaul will be required.

Piston rings worn, weak, broken, or sticking.
Broken or sticking piston rings usually indicate a lubrication or carburation problem that causes excess carbon deposits or seizures to form on the pistons and rings. Top-end overhaul will again be necessary.

Piston ring-to-groove clearance excessive.
This is caused by excessive wear of the piston ring lands. Piston and ring replacement will be called for.

Cylinder head gasket damaged.
If a head is allowed to become loose, or if excessive carbon build-up on the piston crown and combustion chamber causes extremely high compression, the head gasket may leak. Retorquing the head is not always sufficient to restore the seal, so gasket replacement is needed too.

Cylinder head warped.
This is caused by overheating or improperly tightened head bolts. Machine shop resurfacing or head replacement and a new gasket will be needed.

Valve spring broken or weak.
Caused by component failure or wear; the springs must be replaced.

Valve not seating properly.
This is caused by a bent valve (from over-revving or improper valve adjustment), burned valve or seat (improper carburation) or an accumulation of carbon deposits on the seat (from carburation or lubrication problems). The valves must be cleaned and/or replaced and the seats serviced if possible or replaced by an engineering shop.

Stalls after starting

Improper choke action (carburettor models).
See your Haynes manual.

Ignition malfunction.
See your Haynes manual.

Carburettor or fuel injection system malfunction.
See your Haynes manual.

Fuel contaminated.
The fuel can be contaminated with either dirt or water, or can change chemically if the machine is allowed to sit for several months or more. Drain the tank and float chambers. Also check that fuel can flow freely.

Intake air leak.
Check for loose carburettor or throttle body-to-intake manifold connections, loose or missing vacuum gauge adapter screws or hoses, or loose carburettor tops.

Engine idle speed incorrect.
Turn idle adjusting screw until the engine idles at the specified rpm in your manual. On fuel injection models, check other components as specified in your Haynes manual.

Rough idle

Ignition malfunction.
See your Haynes manual.

Idle speed incorrect.
See your Haynes manual.

Carburettors or throttle bodies not synchronised.
Adjust with vacuum gauge or manometer set as described in your Haynes manual.

Carburettor or throttle body or fuel injection system malfunction.
See your Haynes manual.

Fuel contaminated.
The fuel can be contaminated with either dirt or water, or can change chemically if the machine is allowed to sit for several months or more. Drain the tank and float chambers as per your manual.

Intake air leak.
Check for loose carburettor or throttle body-to-intake manifold connections, loose or missing vacuum gauge adaptor screws or hoses, or loose carburettor tops.

Air filter clogged.
Clean or replace the air filter element.

Poor running at low speeds

Spark weak

Battery voltage low.
Check and recharge battery.

Spark plugs fouled, defective or worn out.

Spark plug cap defective.
See your Haynes manual.

Spark plug caps not making contact.

Incorrect spark plugs.
Wrong type, heat range or cap configuration. Check and install correct plugs.

Ignition control unit (carburettor models) or ECM (fuel injection models) defective.
Check as per instructions in your manual.

Pulse generator defective.

Ignition coils defective.

Fuel/air mixture incorrect Carburettor mods

Pilot screws out of adjustment.
See your Haynes manual.

Pilot jet or air passage clogged.
Remove and overhaul the carburettors. See your Haynes manual.

Air bleed holes clogged.
Remove carburettor and blow out all passages. See your Haynes manual.

Fuel level too high or too low.
Check the float height as detailed in your manual.

Carburettor intake manifolds loose.
Check for cracks, breaks, tears or loose clamps. Replace rubber intake manifold joints if split or perished.

Fuel/air mixture incorrect Fuel injection models

Fuel injection system malfunction.
See your Haynes manual.

Fuel injector clogged.
See your Haynes manual.

Fuel pump or pressure regulator faulty.

Throttle body intake manifolds loose.
Check for cracks, breaks, tears or loose clamps. Replace rubber intake manifold joints if split or perished.

Fuel/air mixture incorrect All models

Air filter clogged, poorly sealed or missing.

Air filter housing poorly sealed.
Look for cracks, holes or loose clamps and replace or repair defective parts.

Fuel tank breather hose obstructed.

Compression low

Spark plugs loose.
Remove the plugs and inspect their threads. Reinstall and tighten to the specified torque in your manual.

Cylinder heads not sufficiently tightened down.
If a cylinder head is suspected of being loose, then there's a chance that the gasket and head are damaged if the problem has persisted for any length of time. The head bolts should be tightened to the proper torque in the correct sequence described in your manual.

Incorrect valve clearance.
This means that the valve is not closing completely and compression pressure is leaking past the valve. Check and adjust the valve clearances.

Cylinder and/or piston worn.
Excessive wear will cause compression pressure to leak past the rings. This is usually accompanied by worn rings as well. A top end overhaul is necessary.

Piston rings worn, weak, broken, or sticking.
Broken or sticking piston rings usually indicate a lubrication or carburation problem that causes excess carbon deposits or seizures to form on the pistons and rings. Top-end overhaul is necessary.

Piston ring-to-groove clearance excessive.
This is caused by excessive wear of the piston ring lands. Piston and probably ring replacement is necessary.

Cylinder head gasket damaged.
If a head is allowed to become loose, or if excessive carbon build-up on the piston crown and combustion chamber causes extremely high compression, the head gasket may leak. Retorquing the head is not always sufficient to restore the seal, so gasket replacement is necessary.

Cylinder head warped.
This is caused by overheating or improperly tightened head bolts. Machine shop resurfacing or head replacement is necessary.

Valve spring broken or weak.
Caused by component failure or wear; the springs must be replaced.

Valve not seating properly.
This is caused by a bent valve (from over-revving or improper valve adjustment), burned valve or seat (improper carburation) or an accumulation of carbon deposits on the seat (from carburation, lubrication problems). The valves must be cleaned and/or replaced and the seats recut or replaced if possible.

Poor acceleration

Carburettors or throttle bodies leaking or dirty.
Overhaul them.

Fuel injection system malfunction.
Faulty fuel pump, or pressure regulator (fuel injection models).

Timing not advancing.
The pulse generator or the ignition control unit or ECM may be defective. If so, they must be replaced with new ones, as they can't be repaired.

Carburettors or throttle bodies not synchronised.
Adjust them with a vacuum gauge set or manometer.

Engine oil viscosity too high.
Using a heavier oil than that recommended can damage the oil pump or lubrication system and cause drag on the engine.

Brakes dragging.
Usually caused by debris which has entered the brake piston seals, or from a warped disc or bent wheel spindle. Repair and replace as necessary.

Poor running or no power at high speed

Firing incorrect

Air filter restricted.
Clean or replace filter.

Spark plugs fouled, defective or worn out.

Spark plug caps defective.

Spark plug caps not in good contact.

Incorrect spark plugs.
Wrong type, heat range or cap configuration. Check and install correct plugs listed in your manual.

Ignition control unit or ECM defective.

Ignition coils defective.

Fuel/air mixture incorrect
Carburettor models

Main jet clogged.
Dirt, water or other contaminants can clog the main jets. Clean the fuel tap filter, the in-line filter, the float chamber area, and the jets and carburettor orifices.

Main jet wrong size.
The standard jetting is for sea level atmospheric pressure and oxygen content.

Throttle shaft-to-carb body clearance excessive.
Check manual for inspection and renewal.

Air bleed holes clogged.
Remove carburettor and blow out all passages.

Fuel level too high or too low.
Check the float height.

Carburettor intake manifolds loose.
Check for cracks, breaks, tears or loose clamps. Replace rubber intake manifold joints if split or perished.

Fuel pump, where fitted, faulty.

Fuel/air mixture incorrect
Fuel injection models

Fuel injection system malfunction.

Fuel injector clogged.

Fuel pump or pressure regulator faulty.

Throttle body intake manifolds loose.
Check for cracks, breaks, tears or loose clamps. Replace rubber intake manifold joints if split or perished.

Fuel/air mixture incorrect
All models

Air filter clogged, poorly sealed or missing.

Air filter housing poorly sealed.
Look for cracks, holes or loose clamps and replace or repair defective parts.

Fuel tank breather hose obstructed.

Compression low

Spark plugs loose.
Remove the plugs and inspect their threads. Reinstall and tighten to the specified torque.

Cylinder heads not sufficiently tightened down.
If a cylinder head is suspected of being loose, then there's a chance that the gasket and head are damaged if the problem has persisted for any length of time. The head bolts should be tightened to the proper torque in the correct sequence.

Incorrect valve clearance.
This means that the valve is not closing completely and compression pressure is leaking past the valve. Check and adjust the valve clearances.

Cylinder and/or piston worn.
Excessive wear will cause compression pressure to leak past the rings. This is usually accompanied by worn rings. A top-end overhaul is necessary.

Piston rings worn, weak, broken, or sticking.
Broken or sticking piston rings usually indicate a lubrication or carburation problem that causes excess carbon deposits or seizures to form on the pistons and rings. Top-end overhaul is necessary.

Piston ring-to-groove clearance excessive.
This is caused by excessive wear of the piston ring lands. Piston and probably ring replacement is necessary.

Cylinder head gasket damaged.
If a head is allowed to become loose, or if excessive carbon build-up on the piston crown and combustion chamber causes extremely high compression, the head gasket may leak. Retorquing the head is not always sufficient to restore the seal, so gasket replacement is necessary.

Cylinder head warped.
This is caused by overheating or improperly tightened head bolts. Machine shop resurfacing or head replacement is necessary.

Valve spring broken or weak.
Caused by component failure or wear; the springs must be replaced.

Valve not seating properly.
This is caused by a bent valve (from over-revving or improper valve adjustment), burned valve or seat (improper carburation) or an accumulation of carbon deposits on the seat (from carburation or lubrication problems). The valves must be cleaned and/or replaced and the seats serviced or replaced if possible.

Knocking or pinking

Carbon build-up in combustion chamber.
Use of a fuel additive that will dissolve the adhesive bonding the carbon particles to the crown and chamber is the easiest way to remove the build-up. Otherwise, the cylinder heads will have to be removed and decarbonised. Rare with modern fuels.

Incorrect or poor quality fuel.
Old or improper grades of fuel can cause detonation. This causes the piston to rattle, thus the knocking or pinging sound. Drain old fuel and always use the recommended fuel grade.

Spark plug heat range incorrect.
Uncontrolled detonation indicates the plug heat range is too hot. The plug in effect becomes a glow plug, raising cylinder temperatures. Install the proper heat range plug.

Improper air/fuel mixture.
This will cause the cylinders to run hot, which leads to detonation. Clogged jets or an air leak can cause this imbalance.

Miscellaneous causes

Throttle valve doesn't open fully.
Adjust the throttle grip freeplay.

Clutch slipping.
May be caused by loose or worn clutch components. Refer to your manual for clutch overhaul procedures.

Timing not advancing
Faulty ignition control unit or ECM.

Engine oil viscosity too high.
Using a heavier oil than recommended can damage the oil pump or lubrication system and cause drag on the engine.

Brakes dragging.
Usually caused by debris which has entered the brake piston seals, or from a warped disc or bent axle. Repair and replace as necessary.

Overheating

Engine overheats

Coolant level low.
Check and add coolant.

Leak in cooling system.
Check cooling system hoses and radiator for leaks and other damage. Repair or replace parts as necessary.

Thermostat sticking open or closed.
Check and replace.

Faulty radiator cap.
Remove the cap and have it pressure tested.

Coolant passages clogged.
Have the entire system drained and flushed, then refill with fresh coolant.

Water pump defective.
Remove the pump and check the components.

Clogged radiator fins.
Clean them by blowing compressed air through the fins in the reverse direction of airflow.

Cooling fan or fan switch fault.

Firing incorrect

Spark plugs fouled, defective or worn out.

Incorrect spark plugs.

Ignition control unit or ECM defective.

Pulse generator faulty.

Faulty ignition coils.

Fuel/air mixture incorrect
Carburettor models

Main jet clogged.
Dirt, water or other contaminants can clog the main jets. Clean the fuel tap filter, the in-line filter, the float chamber area, and the jets and carburettor orifices.

Main jet wrong size.
The standard jetting is for sea level atmospheric pressure and oxygen content.

Throttle shaft-to-carburettor body clearance excessive.

Air bleed holes clogged.
Remove carburettor and blow out all passages.

Fuel level too high or too low.
Check the float height.

Carburettor intake manifolds loose.

Check for cracks, breaks, tears or loose clamps. Replace rubber intake manifold joints if split or perished.

Fuel pump faulty.

Fuel/air mixture incorrect
Fuel injection models

Fuel injection system malfunction.

Fuel injector clogged.

Fuel pump or pressure regulator faulty.

Throttle body intake manifolds loose.
Check for cracks, breaks, tears or loose clamps. Replace rubber intake manifold joints if split or perished.

Fuel/air mixture incorrect
All models

Air filter clogged, poorly sealed or missing.

Air filter housing poorly sealed.
Look for cracks, holes or loose clamps and replace or repair defective parts.

Fuel tank breather hose obstructed.

Compression too high

Carbon build-up in combustion chamber.
Use of a fuel additive that will dissolve the adhesive bonding the carbon particles to the piston crown and chamber is the easiest way to remove the build-up. Otherwise, the cylinder heads will have to be removed and decarbonised.

Improperly machined head surface or installation of incorrect gasket during engine assembly.

Engine load excessive

Clutch slipping.
Can be caused by damaged, loose or worn clutch components. Refer to your manual for overhaul procedures.

Engine oil level too high.
The addition of too much oil will cause pressurisation of the crankcase and inefficient engine operation. Check specifications and drain to proper level.

Engine oil viscosity too high.
Using a heavier oil than recommended can damage the oil pump or lubrication system as well as cause drag on the engine.

Brakes dragging.
Usually caused by debris which has entered the brake piston seals, or from a warped disc or bent axle. Repair and replace as necessary.

Lubrication inadequate

Engine oil level too low.
Friction caused by intermittent lack of lubrication or from oil that is overworked can cause overheating. The oil provides a definite cooling function in the engine. Check the oil level.

Poor quality engine oil or incorrect viscosity or type.
Oil is rated not only according to viscosity but also according to type. Some oils are not rated high enough for use in this engine. Check the specifications section in your manual and change to the correct oil.

Miscellaneous causes

Modification to exhaust system.
Most aftermarket exhaust systems cause the engine to run leaner, which makes them run hotter. When installing an accessory exhaust system, always rejet the carburettors or tweak the fuel injection by means of an aftermarket black box. Invest in some dyno time to get the set-up right.

Clutch problems

Clutch slipping

Clutch cable incorrectly adjusted.
Check and adjust.

Friction plates worn or warped.
Overhaul the clutch assembly.

Plain plates warped.

Clutch springs broken or weak.
Old or heat-damaged (from slipping clutch) springs should be replaced with new ones.

Clutch release mechanism defective.
Replace any defective parts.

Clutch centre or housing unevenly worn.
This causes improper engagement of the plates. Replace the damaged or worn parts.

Clutch not disengaging completely

Clutch cable incorrectly adjusted.
Check and adjust.

Clutch plates warped or damaged.
This will cause clutch drag, which in turn will cause the machine to creep. Overhaul the clutch assembly.

Clutch spring tension uneven.
Usually caused by a sagged or broken spring. Check and replace the springs as a set.

Engine oil deteriorated.
Old, thin, worn out oil will not provide proper lubrication for the plates, causing the clutch to drag. Replace the oil and filter.

Engine oil viscosity too high.
Using a heavier oil than recommended can cause the plates to stick together, putting a drag on the engine. Change to the correct weight oil.

Clutch release mechanism defective.

Loose clutch centre nut.
Causes housing and centre misalignment putting a drag on the engine. Engagement adjustment continually varies. Overhaul the clutch assembly.

Gear changing problems

Doesn't go into gear or lever doesn't return.

Clutch not disengaging.
See above.

Selector fork(s) bent or seized.
Often caused by dropping the machine or from lack of lubrication. Overhaul the transmission.

Gear(s) stuck on shaft.
Most often caused by a lack of lubrication or excessive wear in transmission bearings and bushings. Overhaul the transmission.

Selector drum binding.
Caused by lubrication failure or excessive wear. Replace the drum and bearings.

Gearchange lever return spring weak or broken.

Gearchange lever broken.
Splines stripped out of lever or shaft, caused by allowing the lever to get loose or from dropping the machine. Replace necessary parts.

Gearchange mechanism broken or worn.

Jumps out of gear

Selector fork(s) worn.
Overhaul the transmission.

Gear groove(s) worn.
Overhaul the transmission.

Gear dogs or dog slots worn or damaged.
The gears should be inspected and replaced. No attempt should be made to service worn parts.

Abnormal engine noise

Knocking or pinking

Carbon build-up in combustion chamber.
Use of a fuel additive that will dissolve the adhesive bonding the carbon particles to the piston crown and chamber is the easiest way to remove the build-up. Otherwise, the cylinder head will have to be removed and decarbonised. Rare with modern fuels.

Incorrect or poor quality fuel.
Old or improper fuel can cause detonation. This causes the pistons to rattle, thus the knocking or pinging sound. Drain the old fuel and always use the recommended grade.

Spark plug heat range incorrect.
Uncontrolled detonation indicates that the plug heat range is too hot. The plug in effect becomes a glow plug, raising cylinder temperatures. Install the proper heat range plug.

Improper fuel/air mixture.
This will cause the cylinders to run hot and lead to detonation. Clogged jets or an air leak can cause this imbalance.

Piston slap or rattling

Cylinder-to-piston clearance excessive.
Caused by improper assembly. Inspect and overhaul top-end parts.

Connecting rod bent.
Caused by over-revving, trying to start a badly flooded engine or from ingesting a foreign object into the combustion chamber. Replace the damaged parts.

Piston pin or piston pin bore worn or seized from wear or lack of lubrication.
Replace damaged parts.

Piston ring(s) worn, broken or sticking.
Overhaul the top-end.

Piston seizure damage.
Usually from lack of lubrication or overheating. Replace the pistons and have the cylinders rebored as necessary.

Connecting rod upper or lower end clearance excessive.
Caused by excessive wear or lack of lubrication. Replace worn parts.

Valve noise

Incorrect valve clearances.
Adjust the clearances.

Valve spring broken or weak.
Check and replace weak valve springs.

Camshaft or cylinder head worn or damaged.
Lack of lubrication at high rpm is usually the cause of damage. Insufficient oil or failure to change the oil at the recommended intervals are the chief causes.

Other noise

Cylinder head gasket leaking.

Exhaust pipe leaking at cylinder head connection.
Caused by improper fit of pipe(s) or loose exhaust flange. All exhaust fasteners should be tightened evenly and carefully. Failure to do this will lead to a leak.

Crankshaft runout excessive.
Caused by a bent crankshaft (from over-revving) or damage from an upper cylinder component failure. Can also be attributed to dropping the machine on either of the crankshaft ends.

Engine mounting bolts loose.
Tighten all engine mount bolts.

Crankshaft bearings worn.

Camshaft drive assembly defective.

Abnormal clutch noise

Clutch outer drum/friction plate clearance excessive.

Loose or damaged clutch pressure plate and/or bolts.

Transmission noise

Bearings worn.
Also includes the possibility that the shafts are worn. Overhaul the transmission.

Gears worn or chipped.

Metal chips jammed in gear teeth.
Probably pieces from a broken clutch, gear or shift mechanism that were picked up by the gears. This will cause early bearing failure.

Engine oil level too low.
Causes a howl from transmission. Also affects engine power and clutch operation.

Final drive noise

Chain not adjusted properly.

Front or rear sprocket loose.
Tighten fasteners.

Sprockets worn.
Renew sprockets.

Rear sprocket warped.
Renew sprockets.

Rubber dampers in rear wheel hub worn.
Check and renew.

Abnormal frame and suspension noise. Front end noise

Low fluid level or improper viscosity oil in forks.
This can sound like spurting and is usually accompanied by irregular fork action.

Spring weak or broken.
Makes a clicking or scraping sound. Fork oil, when drained, will have a lot of metal particles in it.

Steering head bearings loose or damaged.
Clicks when braking. Check and adjust or replace as necessary.

Fork yokes loose.
Make sure all clamp pinch bolts are tightened to the specified torque.

Fork tube bent.
Good possibility if machine has been dropped. Replace tube with a new one.

Front axle bolt or axle clamp bolts loose.
Tighten them to the specified torque.

Loose or worn wheel bearings.
Check and replace as needed.

Shock absorber noise

Fluid level incorrect.
Indicates a leak caused by defective seal. Shock will be covered with oil. Replace shock or seek advice on repair.

Defective shock absorber with internal damage.
This is in the body of the shock and can't be remedied. The shock must be replaced with a new one.

Bent or damaged shock body.
Replace the shock with a new one.

Loose or worn suspension linkage or swingarm components.
Check and replace as necessary.

Brake noise

Squeal caused by pad shim not installed or positioned correctly (where fitted).

Squeal caused by dust on brake pads.
Usually found in combination with glazed pads. Clean using brake cleaning solvent.

Contamination of brake pads.
Oil, brake fluid or dirt causing brake to chatter or squeal. Clean or replace pads.

Pads glazed. Caused by excessive heat from prolonged use or from contamination.
Do not use sandpaper, emery cloth, carborundum cloth or any other abrasive to roughen the pad surfaces as abrasives will stay in the pad material and damage the disc. A very fine flat file can be used, but pad replacement is suggested as a cure.

Disc warped.
Can cause a chattering, clicking or intermittent squeal. Usually accompanied by a pulsating lever and uneven braking. Replace the disc.

Loose or worn wheel bearings.
Check and replace as required.

Oil pressure indicator light comes on

Engine lubrication system

Engine oil pump defective, blocked oil strainer gauze or failed relief valve.
Carry out oil pressure check as per manual.

Engine oil level low.
Inspect for leak or other problem causing low oil level and add recommended oil.

Engine oil viscosity too low.
Very old, thin oil or an improper weight of oil used in the engine. Change to correct oil.

Camshaft or journals worn.
Excessive wear causing drop in oil pressure. Replace cam and/or cylinder head. Abnormal wear could be caused by oil starvation at high rpm from low oil level or improper weight or type of oil.

Crankshaft and/or bearings worn.
Same problems as above. Check and replace crankshaft and/or bearings.

Electrical system

Oil pressure switch defective.
Check the switch according to the procedure in your manual. Replace it if it is defective.

Oil pressure indicator light circuit defective.
Check for pinched, shorted, disconnected or damaged wiring.

Excessive exhaust smoke

White smoke

Piston oil ring worn.
The ring may be broken or damaged, causing oil from the crankcase to be pulled past the piston into the combustion chamber. Replace the rings with new ones.

Cylinders worn, cracked, or scored.
Caused by overheating or oil starvation. The cylinders will have to be rebored and new pistons installed.

Valve oil seal damaged or worn.
Replace oil seals with new ones.

Valve guide worn.
Perform, or have performed, a complete valve job.

Engine oil level too high, which causes the oil to be forced past the rings.
Drain oil to the proper level.

Head gasket broken between oil return and cylinder.
Causes oil to be pulled into the combustion chamber. Replace the head gasket and check the head for warpage.

Abnormal crankcase pressurisation, which forces oil past the rings.
Clogged breather is usually the cause.

Black smoke
Carburettor models

Main jet too large or loose.
Compare the jet size to the Specifications in your manual.

Choke cable or linkage shaft stuck, causing fuel to be pulled through choke circuit.

Fuel level too high.
Check and adjust the float height(s) as necessary.

Float needle valve held off needle seat.
Clean the float chambers and fuel line and replace the needles and seats if necessary.

Black smoke
Fuel injection models

Fuel injection system malfunction.

Black smoke
All models

Air filter clogged.

Brown smoke
Carburettor models

Main jet too small or clogged.
Lean condition caused by wrong size main jet or by a restricted orifice. Clean float chambers and jets and compare jet size to Specifications in your manual.

Fuel flow insufficient.
Float needle valve stuck closed due to chemical reaction with old fuel. Float height incorrect. Restricted fuel line. Clean line and float chamber and adjust floats if necessary.

Carburettor intake manifold clamps loose.

Faulty fuel pump.

Brown smoke
Fuel injection models

Fuel injection system malfunction.

Faulty fuel pump or pressure regulator.

Brown smoke
All models

Air filter poorly sealed or not installed.

Poor handling or stability

Handlebar hard to turn

Steering head bearing adjuster nut too tight.
Check adjustment as described in your manual.

Bearings damaged.
Roughness can be felt as the bars are turned from side-to-side. Replace bearings and races.

Races dented or worn.
Denting results from wear in only one position (e.g. straight ahead), from a collision or hitting a pothole or from dropping the machine. Replace races and bearings. Steering stem lubrication inadequate. Causes are grease getting hard from age or being washed out by high pressure car washes. Disassemble steering head and repack and/or replace bearings.

Steering stem bent.
Caused by a collision, hitting a pothole or by dropping the machine. Replace damaged part. Don't try to straighten the steering stem.

Front tyre air pressure too low.

Handlebar shakes or vibrates excessively

Tyres worn, out of balance or at incorrect pressures.

Swingarm bearings worn.
Replace worn bearings.

Wheel rim(s) warped or damaged.
Inspect wheels for runout.

Wheel bearings worn.
Worn front or rear wheel bearings can cause poor tracking. Worn front bearings will cause wobble.

Handlebar clamp bolts loose.

Fork yoke bolts loose.
Tighten them to the specified torque in your manual.

Engine mounting bolts loose.
Will cause excessive vibration with increased engine rpm.

Handlebar pulls to one side

Frame bent.
Definitely suspect this if the machine has been dropped. May or may not be accompanied by cracking near the bend. Replace the frame if it can't be safely straightened.

Wheels out of alignment.
Caused by improper location of spindle spacers or from bent steering stem or frame.

Swingarm bent or twisted.
Caused by age (metal fatigue) or impact damage. Replace the arm.

Steering stem bent.
Caused by impact damage or by dropping the motorcycle. Replace steering stem.

Fork tube bent.
Disassemble the forks and replace the damaged parts.

Fork oil level uneven.
Check and add or drain as necessary.

Poor shock absorbing qualities

Too hard:
a) Fork oil level excessive.
b) Fork oil viscosity too high. Use a lighter oil (see the Specifications in your manual).
c) Fork tube bent. Causes a harsh, sticking feeling.
d) Shock shaft or body bent or damaged.
e) Fork internal damage.
f) Shock internal damage.
g) Tyre pressure too high.
h) Suspension adjusters incorrectly set

Too soft:
a) Fork or shock oil insufficient and/or leaking.
b) Fork oil level too low.
c) Fork oil viscosity too light.
d) Fork springs weak or broken.
e) Shock internal damage or leakage.
f) Suspension adjusters incorrectly set

Braking problems

Brakes are spongy, or lack power

Air in brake line.
Caused by inattention to master cylinder fluid level or by leakage. Locate problem and bleed brakes. Cable problem on drum brakes.

Pad or disc (or drum/shoes) worn.

Brake fluid leak.

Contaminated pads/shoes.
Caused by contamination with oil, grease, brake fluid, etc. Clean or replace. Clean disc/drum thoroughly with brake cleaner.

Brake fluid deteriorated.
Fluid is old or contaminated. Drain system, replenish with new fluid and bleed the system.

Master cylinder internal parts worn or damaged causing fluid to bypass.

Master cylinder bore scratched by foreign material or broken spring.
Repair or replace master cylinder.

Disc warped/drum out of true.
Replace disc/drum.

Brake lever or pedal pulsates

Disc warped/drum out of true.
Replace/skim.

Spindle bent.
Replace spindle.

Brake caliper bolts loose.

Brake caliper sliders damaged or sticking (rear caliper), causing caliper to bind.
Lubricate the sliders or replace them if they are corroded or bent.

Wheel warped or otherwise damaged.

Wheel bearings damaged or worn.

Brakes drag

Master cylinder piston seized.
Caused by wear or damage to piston or cylinder bore. Incorrect cable/rod/shoe adjustment on drum systems.

Lever sticky or stuck.
Check pivot and lubricate.

Brake caliper binds on bracket (rear caliper).
Caused by inadequate lubrication or damage to caliper sliders.

Brake caliper piston seized in bore.
Caused by wear or ingestion of dirt past deteriorated seal.

Brake pad/shoe damaged.
Pad/shoe material separated from backing plate. Usually caused by faulty manufacturing process or from contact with chemicals. Replace.

Pads/shoes improperly installed.

Electrical problems

Battery dead or weak

Battery faulty.
Caused by sulphated plates which are shorted through sedimentation. Also, broken battery terminal making only occasional contact.

Battery cables making poor contact.

Load excessive.
Caused by addition of high wattage lights or other electrical accessories.

Ignition (main) switch defective.
Switch either grounds (earths) internally or fails to shut off system. Replace the switch.

Regulator/rectifier defective.

Alternator stator coil open or shorted.

Wiring faulty.
Wiring grounded (earthed) or connections loose in ignition, charging or lighting circuits.

Battery overcharged

Regulator/rectifier defective.
Overcharging is noticed when battery gets excessively warm.

Battery defective.
Replace battery with a new one.

Battery amperage too low, wrong type or size.
Install manufacturer's specified amp-hour battery to handle charging load.

Glossary

A

Accelerator pump A carburettor device for temporarily increasing the amount of fuel.

Air filter Either a paper, fabric, felt, foam or gauze element through which the engine draws its air.

Air/fuel ratio Proportions in which air and fuel are mixed to form a combustible gas.

Alternator A generator of alternating current (a.c.) electricity.

ABS (Anti-lock braking system) A system that prevents the wheels locking up under braking.

Ampere-hour (Ah) Measure of battery capacity.

Antifreeze A substance (usually ethylene glycol) mixed with water, and added to the cooling system, to prevent freezing of the coolant in winter.

Anti-dive System attached to the fork lower leg (slider) to prevent fork dive when braking hard.

Aspect ratio With a tyre, the ratio of the section's depth to its width.

ATF Automatic Transmission Fluid. Often used in front forks.

Axle A shaft on which a wheel revolves. Also known as a spindle.

B

Backlash The amount of movement between meshed components. Usually applies to gear teeth.

Ball bearing A bearing consisting of a hardened inner and outer race with hardened steel balls between the two races.

BDC Bottom Dead Centre – denotes that the piston is at the lowest point of its stroke in the cylinder.

Bearings Used between two working surfaces to prevent wear of the components and a build-up of heat.

Belt drive Drive by a belt. Typical applications are for drive to the camshafts and transmission, and sometimes to the rear wheel.

Bevel gear Gear with slanted teeth, a pair of such gears turning the drive through ninety degrees.

BHP Brake horsepower.

Bias-belted tyre Similar construction to radial tyre, but with outer belt running at an angle to the wheel rim.

Big-end The larger end of a connecting rod and the one mounted on the crankpin.

Bleeding The process of removing air from an hydraulic system.

Bore Diameter of a cylinder.

Bore:stroke ratio The ratio of cylinder diameter to stroke. When these are equal the engine is said to be square.

Bottom Dead Centre (BDC) Lowest point of piston's stroke in the cylinder.

Bottom-end An engine's crankcase components and all components contained there-in.

BTDC Before Top Dead Centre in terms of piston position. Ignition timing is often expressed in terms of degrees or millimetres BTDC.

Bush A cylindrical metal and/or rubber component used between two moving parts.

C

Caliper In an hydraulic brake system, the component spanning the disc and housing the pistons and brake pads.

Cam chain The chain which takes drive from the crankshaft to the camshaft(s).

Cam follower A component in contact with the camshaft lobes, transmitting motion to the valve gear.

Camshaft A rotary shaft for the operation of valve gear in poppet valve engines.

Carburettor Mixes variable volumes of air and fuel in the correct ratio.

Catalytic converter A device in the exhaust system of some machines which converts certain pollutants in the exhaust gases into less harmful substances.

Centrifugal To be thrown outwards. An outward force on an object moving around a point.

Charging system Description of the components which charge the battery.

Clutch A device for engaging or disengaging the engine from the driving wheel.

Coil spring A spiral of elastic steel.

Compression Squeezing smaller, particularly a fresh charge of mixture in the cylinder by the rising piston.

Compression damping Controls the speed the suspension compresses when hitting a bump.

Compression ratio The extent to which the contents of the cylinder are compressed by the rising piston.

Concentric Tending to a common centre.

Connecting-rod The rod connecting the piston to the crankshaft via the big and small ends.

Constant rate A spring is this when each equal increment in load produces an equal change in length. (Contrast with multi-rate and progressive rate.)

Crankcase The chamber which carries the crankshaft.

Crankshaft A forged component, using the principle of the eccentric (crank) for converting the reciprocating piston engine's linear power pulse into rotary motion.

Cross-ply tyre Form of tyre construction in which the wraps of fabric in the tyre carcass are laid over each other diagonally instead of radially (see radial ply).

Cush drive A shock-absorbing component in a transmission system.

Cylinder head Component closing the blind end of the cylinder. Houses the valve gear on a four-stroke engine.

D

Damper A device for controlling and perhaps eliminating unwanted movement in suspension systems.

Detonation Explosion of the mixture in the combustion chamber, instead of controlled burning. May cause a tinkling noise, known as pinking, under an open throttle.

Diaphragm The rubber membrane in a master cylinder or carburettor which seals the upper chamber.

Disc brake A brake design incorporating a rotating disc onto which the brake pads are squeezed.

Displacement The amount of volume displaced by the piston of an engine on rising from its lowest position to its highest.

Dog A projection from a moving part, mating with another dog or a slot. Used in gearboxes to connect two pinions on a shaft.

Double-overhead camshaft (DOHC) An engine that uses two overhead camshafts, one for the intake valves and one for the exhaust valves.

Downdraught Downward inclination of the induction tract, usually the carburettor too.

Dry sump Four-stroke lubrication system in which the oil is carried in a separate oil tank and not in the sump.

Duplex Two. A duplex frame has two front down tubes. A duplex chain has two rows of rollers (a simple chain has one).

E

Earth Usually the negative terminal of a battery, or part of the earth return.

Earth return The path of an electrical circuit that returns to the battery, utilising the motorcycle's frame.

ECU (Electronic Control Unit) A computer which controls (for instance) an ignition system, or an anti-lock braking system.

EMS (Engine Management System) A computer controlled system which manages the fuel injection and the ignition systems.

Expansion chamber Section of two-stroke engine exhaust system so designed to improve engine efficiency and boost power.

F

Final drive Description of the drive from the transmission to the rear wheel. Usually by chain or shaft, but sometimes by belt.

Firing order The order in which the engine cylinders fire, or deliver their power strokes, beginning with the number one cylinder.

Flat twin (or four/six) An engine with horizontal adjacent or opposed cylinders, thereby having a flat configuration.

Float A buoyant object. Used in a carburettor to open and close the fuel inlet valve to maintain a constant fuel level.

Float chamber A carburettor component used to stabilise the fuel level in the carb.

Float level The height at which the float is positioned in the float chamber, so determining the fuel level.

Flywheel A rotating mass of considerable weight and radius, used to smooth out power impulses at the crank.

Four-stroke An operating cycle for an internal combustion engine in which combustion takes place on every other ascent of the piston. See also Two-stroke.

Freeplay The amount of travel before any action takes place, for example, the distance the rear brake pedal moves before the rear brake is actuated.

Friction The resistance between two bodies moving in contact with each other and relatively to each other.

Front fork Telescopic tubes incorporating springs and dampers used to provide a suspension system for the front of a motorcycle.

Fuel injection The fuel/air mixture is metered electronically and directed into the engine intake ports (indirect injection) or into the cylinders (direct injection). Sensors supply information on engine speed and conditions.

Fuel/air mixture The charge of fuel and air going into the engine.

Fuel level The level of fuel in a float chamber. Can be altered by changing the float level.

Fulcrum The point about which a leverage system pivots.

Fuse An electrical device which protects a circuit against accidental overload.

G

Gasket Any thin, soft material – usually cork, cardboard, asbestos or soft metal – installed between two metal surfaces to ensure a good seal.

Gear A component, often circular, with projections for the positive transmission of movement to a companion gear which may, or may not be, of the same shape and size.

Gearbox An assembly containing the transmission components used in varying the ratio of the gearing.

Gear ratio The ratio of turning speeds of any pair of gears or sprockets, derived from their number of teeth.

Gudgeon pin The pin, usually made of hardened steel, linking the piston to the small end of the connecting rod.

H

Helical gears Gear teeth are slightly curved and produce less noise than straight-cut gears. Often used for primary drives.

HT High Tension Description of the electrical circuit from the secondary winding of the ignition coil to the spark plug.

HT lead A heavily insulated wire carrying the high tension current from the coil to the spark plug.

Horizontally-opposed A type of engine in which the cylinders are opposite to each other with the crankshaft in between.

Hub The centre part of a wheel.

Hydraulic A liquid-filled system used to transmit pressure from one component to another. Common uses on motorcycles are brake and clutch actuating mechanisms.

Hygroscopic Water absorbing. In motorcycle applications, braking efficiency will be reduced if DOT 3 or 4 hydraulic fluid absorbs water from the air – care must be taken to keep new brake fluid in tightly sealed containers.

Hypoid oil An extreme-pressure oil formulated to stand up to severe and unique conditions in hypoid transmission gears.

I

lbf ft Pounds-force feet. An imperial unit of torque. Sometimes written as ft-lbs.

Ignition advance Means of increasing the timing of the spark at higher engine speeds. Done by mechanical means on early engines or electronically by the ignition control unit on later engines.

Ignition timing The moment at which the spark plug fires, expressed in the number of crankshaft degrees before the piston reaches the top of its stroke, or in the number of millimetres before the piston reaches the top of its stroke.

Injector Equipment for squirting a fluid. Used for both fuel and oil.

Inverted forks (upside down forks) The sliders or lower legs are held in the yokes and the fork tubes or stanchions are connected to the wheel axle (spindle). Less unsprung weight and stiffer construction than conventional forks.

J

Jet A hole through which air, fuel or oil passes, the size of the jet determining the quantity.

Joule The unit of electrical energy.

K

Kickstart A crank, operated by foot, for starting an engine.

Knock Similar to detonation, with same end results, but only the end gases in the far reaches of the combustion chamber ignite. The knocking sound, also known as pinking, occurs when the central and outer flame fronts meet.

L

Lambda (λ) sensor A sensor fitted in the exhaust system to measure the exhaust gas oxygen content (excess air factor).

Land The raised portion between two grooves (e.g. between the ring grooves in a piston).

Layshaft In a 'direct top gearbox' a gearbox shaft parallel to the mainshaft and carrying the laygears with which the mainshaft gears mesh to achieve ratio change.

Leading link A form of front suspension using a pivoting link – approximately horizontal – with the axle in front of the pivot.

LT Low Tension Description of the electrical circuit from the power supply to the primary winding of the ignition coil.

Lubricant A substance, usually an oil, interposed between rubbing surfaces to decrease friction.

M

Main bearing The principal bearing(s) on which a component is carried but usually reserved exclusively for the crankshaft.

Mainshaft A principal shaft, as in an engine or a gearbox.

Master cylinder The operator end of an hydraulic control system.

Monoshock A single suspension unit linking the swingarm or suspension linkage to the frame.

Multigrade oil Having a wide viscosity range (e.g. 10W40). The viscosity ranges from SAE10 when cold to SAE40 when hot.

Multi-rate A spring which changes length unequally for equal increments of load. (Contrast with constant rate and progressive rate.)

N

Needle roller bearing A bearing made up of many small diameter rollers of hardened steel, usually kept separated by a cage. Often used where lubrication is poor.

Negative earth Using the negative or minus pole of the battery as the earth.

Nm Newton metres used to measure torque.

O

Odometer A mileage recorder.

Oil injection A system of two-stroke engine lubrication where oil is pump-fed to the engine in accordance with throttle position.

Oil pump A mechanically-driven device for distributing oil around a four-stroke engine or pumping oil into a two-stroke engine.

Overhead valve (OHV) A four-stroke engine with the valves in the cylinder head and operated by pushrods.

Overhead cam (OHC) As above but with the camshaft contained in the cylinder head and operated by chain, gear or belt from the crankshaft.

P

Pinking The noise arising from Detonation and Knock.

Pitch The nominal distance between two specified points such as gear teeth, spring coils or chain rollers.

Plug cap A cover over the top of a spark plug that transmits the HT voltage from the coil and lead to the plug.

Plug lead A heavily insulated wire carrying the high tension current from the coil to the spark plug.

Port Strictly, a hole or opening but also used to described the transfer ports in a two-stroke engine.

Power band The band of rpm in which the engine produces really useful power.

Pre-ignition Auto-ignition taking place before the desired moment and happening, not by sparking, but by incandescence.

Pre-load (suspension) The amount a spring is compressed when in the unloaded state. Pre-load can be adjusted by gas, spacer or mechanical adjuster. Determines ride height.

Premix The method of engine lubrication on older two-stroke engines. Engine oil is mixed with the petrol in the fuel tank in a specific ratio.

Primary gears The pair of gears connecting the crankshaft to the clutch in a unit construction engine.

Progressive rate A spring that progressively deflects less for equal increments in load (see Constant rate and Multi-rate).

Pushrod A stout rod used to transmit a push as in clutch or overhead-valve operation.

R

Radial ply tyre Form of tyre construction in which the wraps of fabric in the tyre carcass are laid over each other radially, and not diagonally.

Radiator Device for losing heat.

Rake The angle of the steering axis from the vertical.

Rebore Removing the worn surface of a cylinder to create a new working surface.

Rebound damping A means of controlling the oscillation of a suspension unit spring after it has been compressed.

Rectifier Electrical device passing current in one direction only (and thus a wave), used to convert alternating current into direct current.

Reed valves A valve functioning like a reed, with pressure causing the 'flap' to open or close.

Regulator Device for maintaining the charging voltage from the generator or alternator within a specified range.

Relay An electrical device used to switch heavy current on and off using a low current auxiliary circuit. Relays are used to switch heavy currents such as for the starter motor.

Rim The edge, margin or periphery. In the case of a wheel, the part that carries the tyre.

Rising rate Condition set up using a three-way linkage between the swingarm and the shock absorber to give progressive suspension action.

Roller bearing One containing rollers as the support medium, and not balls.

rpm Revolutions per minute.

S

Seizure The binding together of two moving parts through pressure, temperature or lack of lubrication, and often all three.

Shaft drive A method of transmitting drive from the transmission to the rear wheel.

Shock absorber A device for ironing out the effects of riding over bumps in the road to give a smooth ride.

Single-overhead camshaft (SOHC) An engine that uses one overhead camshaft to operate both intake valves and exhaust valves via rockers.

Small-end The smaller end on a connecting rod to which the piston is attached.

Spark plug Device for arcing an electric current, as a spark, between two electrodes inserted in the combustion space.

Spindle The fixed rod about which an article turns or perhaps swings in an arc.

Sprocket Toothed wheel used in chain drive.

Stanchion In a telescopic front fork, that tubular part attached to the fork yokes and on or in which travels the moving slider.

Steering head The part of the frame which houses the steering stem.

Stroke The distance between the highest and lowest points of the piston's travel.

Sub-frame The rear part of a motorcycle frame which carries the seat, rear lighting and electrical components.

Sump Chamber on the bottom of a four-stroke engine that contains the oil.

Swingarm Supports the rear wheel and rear suspension.

T

Taper rollerbearing A hardened steel roller, being tapered instead of cylindrical.

Tachometer Rev-counter.

Thermostat Controls the flow of engine coolant into the radiator.

Timing The opening and closing points of valves and the moment of ignition in the engine cycle.

Top Dead Centre (TDC) Highest point of a piston's stroke.

Top-end A description of an engine's cylinder block, head and valve gear components.

Torque A twisting force about a shaft, measured in Nm, kgf m or lbf ft.

Trail The distance between the point where a vertical line through the wheel axle touches the ground, and the point where a line through the steering axis touches the ground.

Twistgrip Rotary throttle control on the right handlebar, operated by twisting.

Two-stroke An operating cycle for an internal combustion engine in which combustion takes place on every ascent of the piston. The four events (induction, compression, ignition, exhaust) in the engine cycle are thus completed in two strokes (one up, one down) of the piston. See also Four-stroke.

U

Unsprung weight Anything not supported by the bike's suspension (i.e. the wheel, tyres, brakes, final drive and bottom (moving) part of the suspension).

Upside down forks (inverted forks) In contrast to conventional forks, these have the inner tube at the bottom, connected to the wheel axle, and acting as the slider, moving in the outer tube.

V

Valve A device through which the flow of liquid, gas or vacuum may be stopped, started or regulated by a movable part that opens, shuts or partially obstructs one or more ports or passageways. The intake and exhaust valves in the cylinder head are of the poppet type.

Valve seat That part of the cylinder head against which the valve face seats and seals.

V-engine A motor with its cylinders arranged in V formation.

W

Watercooling Engine cooling system which uses a recirculating liquid coolant which passes through channels in the engine castings and externally through a radiator.

Water pump A mechanically-driven device for moving coolant around the engine.

Wet sump Conventional four-stroke engine lubrication system in which the oil is carried in a pan (sump) on the bottom of the crankcase.

Wheelbase The distance, between the axles of the front and rear wheels.

Y

Yokes Connect the steering stem to the front forks.

Index

Photos:
Tom Critchell,
John Noble,
Phillip Tooth,
Aprilia, BMW, CCM,
Ducati, Harley-Davidson,
Honda, Hyperbolt, Italjet,
Kawasaki, KTM, Suzuki,
Triumph, Yamaha

**Author
Acknowledgements:**
Bob Gray
the late John Robinson,
Louise McIntyre,
Simon Larkin,
Luke Brackenbury,
Tom Critchell (again)
Lisa and Esme
Mark Brewin
Trevor Franklin
Garry Coull

Written by
Alan Seeley
Design
Simon Larkin
Technical editor
Martynn Randall
Editor
Peter McSean
Project Manager
Louise McIntyre